BEING THERE

BEING THERE

MEMOIR OF AN ASIAN AMERICAN JOURNALIST

LORI MATSUKAWA

Published by:

Chin Music Press
1501 Pike Place #329
Seattle, WA 98101-1542
www.chinmusicpress.com

First edition

Library of Congress Control Number: 2026938630

ISBN: 9781634051064

Printed in the USA

Cover photo by Alan Alabastro

ALSO BY LORI MATSUKAWA

Brave Mrs. Sato

Chin Music Press, Seattle

Copyright 2023

Intersections: A Journalistic History of

Asian Pacific America

Co-editor, Contributor

Asian American Journalists Association in partnership with UCLA,

Asian American Studies Center

Copyright 2025

To my husband, Larry L. Blackstock, who has always believed in me, even when I didn't believe in myself. Our son, Alexander S. Blackstock, who continues to astonish me to this day. And to my parents, Joe S. and Florence E. Matsukawa, who encouraged my sisters and me to live the American Dream and honor those who prepared the way.

CHAPTER 1
ON THE RADIO

The heart-stopping sound came over the radio, the half-telegraph, half-flute doodle that meant something IMPORTANT was going to be announced. Was it a shooting? A tsunami warning?

That November afternoon in 1973, the disc jockey opened the microphone and announced breathlessly, "Lori Lei Matsukawa of Aiea has just been named Miss Teenage America in Fort Worth, Texas!"

George Carter, a local businessman, was driving along H-1, Honolulu's main highway and pounded his steering wheel.

"Yes! She did it!" he crowed. Carter lived in Aiea and considered Lori the "daughter he never had."

Meanwhile, the DJ called Lori's parents. Her mom, Florence, answered.

"Mrs. Matsukawa, your daughter has just been named Miss Teenage America! How do you feel?"

"What? She did? Daddy! Come over here and talk to this man. Lori just won the contest!" She covered the receiver and hollered at her husband Joe, who was just heading out the door to a University of Hawaii football game.

"She what?" listeners could hear him in the background.

Such was the pandemonium on that crazy afternoon which would be a seismic event in my life.

JUST HOURS BEFORE MY PARENTS' lives were so unexpectedly interrupted, I had been standing on a stage in Fort Worth showered by streamers and surrounded by screaming young women congratulating me on winning my national title. The CBS announcer was signing off the broadcast and Ellie, my chaperone, quietly slipped out of her seat and headed to our hotel room to pack our things. We had a plane to New York to catch.

While Mom and Dad were winging their way to the Miss Teenage America headquarters in Dallas, I was on a flight to New York to appear on the Dr Pepper float in the Macy's Thanksgiving Day parade.

New York was a blur. Somewhere along the way to the float Ellie and I shared an elevator with television actor William Conrad who played a detective in "Cannon." He eyed my "Miss Teenage America" sash.

"Congratulations," he smiled. I smiled back. "Thank you. So nice to meet you."

What a goofy thing for me to say, I thought.

All I remember of the parade was wearing thermal under-wear and God-awful black rain boots under my parade gown and shivering as the float crawled down Sixth Avenue.

"Smile and wave," were the last things I heard from Ellie as she pulled gloves over my frozen digits. She was a profes-sional model, so she knew how to keep to the program.

I smiled my most dazzling smile for two hours straight, waving to a blur of cheering faces along the streets of New York. I was shivering from the cold and from excitement. "Is this really happening??" I kept thinking.

"How can this be?" I said softly under my breath. "I was

the ugly duckling. The kid with glasses and braces and knock knees and no boyfriend. How is this happening?"

The next day, Mom, Dad, Ellie and I were sitting across the desk from Charles R. Meeker, Jr., the President of the Miss Teenage America franchise. A heavy-set man in an impeccable navy suit, he sized me up with his VERY blue eyes.

"You'll be traveling a lot and making several public appearances. You may be asked to do speeches." He ticked through what we could expect through the upcoming year. Orange Bowl, Kentucky Derby, Indianapolis 500 parades, bottling plant ribbon cuttings (our main sponsor was the Dr Pepper company), you get to pick out ten new outfits each season from Jerrell (another sponsor)."

Mom looked at me and her eyes got wide. I looked at her and Dad and my eyes got wider. It's a lot to take in when you're just seventeen.

"Do you think you'll be able to handle your school work and graduate this year?" Mr. Meeker wrapped up. I nodded.

"No problem. I only need a few credits in English and Social Studies," I replied, though I really hadn't asked my teachers yet.

"Any questions?" he smiled and suddenly he looked quite fatherly.

"Will I have any problem because I'm Japanese? I mean, I don't look like the usual Miss Teenage America," I asked intently.

I was the thirteenth Miss Teenage America for the franchise, the first non-white girl to be selected. At the contest last week, there had been several candidates of color — Puerto Rican, African American, Chinese American — but who would have guessed the job would go to a Japanese American girl who attended public school in Hawaii?

Mr. Meeker looked determined.

"I don't think you'll have any problem at all," he said.

"You're an All-American girl from Hawai'i. If anything at all happens, you let us know."

CHAPTER 2
HOW DID I GET HERE?

am always amazed that a family can go from non-English speaking immigrants to Miss Teenage America to television journalist in the span of sixty-five years. Three generations, boom! Such is America.

My father's father, my grandfather, Masaji Matsukawa, came to Kaua'i, Hawai'i, from Niigata, Japan in 1904 as a nineteen-year-old to work in the cane fields near Kekaha Camp. Because he could read and write, he became a liaison between the camp and the Japanese Consulate in Honolulu. He recorded births, deaths, arrivals and departures. This may be the reason he was put in detention first at Wailua Camp, then Kalaheo Camp after the Japanese attacked Pearl Harbor in December 1941. He was released for medical reasons several months later. He and his wife, Akino Hashii, raised eight children. My dad, Joe Sadao, was the youngest and the only one born at a hospital.

My mother's father, my grandfather, Shogoro Shimizu, came to Honolulu, Hawai'i, from Hiroshima, Japan, in 1904 at the age of sixteen. He initially worked as a yard boy and "servant" for a Caucasian man who managed pineapple fields. He then worked on a local dairy farm and later, struck out on his own to become a prosperous dairy farmer near Diamond Head. Because he was important to the "war effort," he and his three sons were not incarcerated in camps during World War II. In fact, they had all the gasoline they needed and none of the young men was drafted. Shogoro married his wife, my grandmother Hatsumi Oda, two days after she stepped off the S.S. Manchuria in Honolulu at the age of nineteen in 1914. She was a "picture bride" — set up by a matchmaker in Japan after exchanging photos with Shogoro. Shogoro and Hatsumi raised eight children. My mom, Florence Eiko, was the youngest.

My parents met at the University of Hawai'i. By then, they pretty much used their English names, which they selected themselves at the request of their elementary school teachers who were white and couldn't pronounce Japanese names. My mom named herself Florence, after Florence Nightingale. She graduated in 1953 with a primary education degree. She was the only one of the eight children in her family to go to the UH. My dad, Joe, named himself after New York Yankee "Joltin'" Joe DiMaggio. He attended the UH on an athletic scholarship (He was the school's star quarterback and appeared in the Hula Bowl in 1954. He played baseball, too). He also had an ROTC scholarship. He graduated in 1954 with a degree in Physical Education. Of the eight children in his family, just he and an older sister went to the university. Five of the siblings remained on Kaua'i with their widowed mother.

When I asked Dad why he married Mom, he said she was kind. When I asked Mom why she married Dad, she said he respected his mother and that bode well for whoever would become his wife. Only later in their marriage did Mom add that a Japanese matchmaker once told her mother that Joe's sister married a Morisato and if that sister was good enough for a Morisato, then Joe was good enough for Florence!

Joe and Flo married on June 18, 1955, at Star of the Sea

Church in Manoa. Mom had a beautiful lace gown with a nineteen-inch waist. When I tried to wear the gown as a high school sophomore, I couldn't button it up. They quickly moved to Fort Ord, California, where Dad went to basic training to fulfill his ROTC obligations. They came back to Hawai'i a year later. That's where I was born on July 7, 1956.

As a *Sansei*, third-generation Japanese American, I grew up pushed forward and pulled back. Pushed forward by an American society bursting with change. The voting rights movement, the civil rights movement, immigration reform, the Cold War, the Vietnam War, the war on poverty, the women's movement, the peace movement, the summer of love, the assassinations of John Kennedy, Martin Luther King Jr. and Robert Kennedy, the space race. Pulled back by cultural values from old Japan like *on*, obligation to one's parents and society with a self-sacrificing devotion. And *haji*, shame that must never come upon one's reputation and family name.

Cultural values, too precious to cast away. Push, pull. Looking back, I realize my *Nisei*, second-generation parents were struggling to bridge the cultural divide as best as they could. Joe Sadao and Florence Eiko admonished their three daughters with Hawaiian middle names to "Listen to your parents! Get good grades! Be pretty but don't get pregnant! Be self-sufficient but not too self-sufficient, men can't deal with that! Don't break the law! People will talk about you behind your back, so don't give them a reason to! Don't shame the family name!"

Fear of what others would think became a major motivator in my life. Without the benign nurturing Hawaiian culture surrounding me, I would have drowned.

CHAPTER 3
A RISING TIDE
LIFTS ALL BOATS

When I was born, Hawai'i was still a territory of the United States. Statehood wouldn't come until August 21, 1959. It was a booming time in Hawai'i. Many *Nisei* men who returned from World War II went to college on the G.I. Bill. They got steady jobs in education, government or ran their own businesses. They got married and started raising middle-class families.

There is little doubt in my mind that living as part of a large immigrant community on islands in the middle of the Pacific helped generate optimism and confidence in the Japanese descendants living there. According to the book *Okage sama de — The Japanese in Hawaii*, the Japanese comprised a third of the territory's population in 1941 (approximately 160,000: 120,000 citizens and 40,000 aliens). They had many Caucasian supporters who saw them as loyal and essential to the war effort. Among them, Honolulu Police Captain John A. Burns, who grew up with Japanese in Hawai'i and would later become the governor after statehood. Burns vouched for their loyalty to the F.B.I. Special Agent in Charge, Robert L. Shivers, who concluded that the majority were loyal to America and there was no need to ruin people's lives by locking them up in camps like so many other people of Japanese descent on the Mainland.

After the War, despite hardship and racism endured by the *Issei* (my grandparents' generation), my parents' generation, the *Nisei*, were bursting to create the best opportunities for THEIR children, the *Sansei*. I grew up taking for granted that Japanese Americans were teachers, bankers, members of Congress and newscasters.

In my young baby-brain, I just assumed everyone had two parents who both worked and could afford to drive a beater car. Dad taught social studies at Leilehua High School and mom taught kindergarten at Wahiawa Elementary. In the morning before the school bell rang, mom dropped me off at my babysitter's house. Mrs. June Tara (I called her Aunty Tara — in Hawai'i, every woman your mom's age or older was called Aunty as a sign of respect) was like a younger version of my grandmothers. She wore belted cotton shifts in dull gray or blue prints, a hairnet and spoke "for real" Pidgin English. In my baby-brain, I thought everyone spoke Pidgin — a mix of Japanese, English and Hawaiian.

"Rori, no run *hadashi* (barefoot in Japanese). Your clothes all *kapakahi* (crooked in Hawaiian)! *Jamaninaru!*" (You're in the way in Japanese).

Hawai'i's rich mix of ethnic groups was a true gift. There was respect for others' traditions and cuisine. Because every group was a "minority," we all did our best to get along. My first-grade teacher was a large Hawaiian/Chinese woman named Mrs. Yong. Each morning, she stood in front of the room, rested her tiny ukulele on her shelf-like bosom and led the class in singing "America the Beautiful." Considering I was the daughter of two school teachers, I think she couldn't believe that I had never seen a "Dick and Jane" book until the morning she opened one in class. The other kids around me on the floor seemed to know how to read. But I didn't. Same thing with addition. When Mrs. Yong wrote 1+1=2 on the chalkboard, I had NO IDEA what it was. The last embarrassment to my parents that year was my first "research" paper. I just thought I had to tell the class what I knew about Johnny Appleseed.

"Johnny Appleseed liked to plant apple trees," I wrote, trying to recall scenes from Walt Disney's cartoon about the legendary arborist. "He had animal friends and people friends, too." That was it. Of course, my classmates had done ACTUAL research and knew his name was John Chapman born on September 26, 1774, in Massachusetts. Later, Mrs. Yong told my mother (who was teaching in the next wing over) that she thought I might be a little "slow." I felt sheepish and vowed to do better.

In the second grade, I tried to up my academic game. I had a Japanese teacher named Miss Matsuda. I was often frustrated in her class because she made us copy things she wrote on the chalkboard. I told her I already knew what the sentences meant, so why did I have to write them down? She told me to "just do what I ask." When President Kennedy was shot, Miss Matsuda put her head down on her desk and wept. All the kids in class were shocked; some girls even started crying, too. I never challenged her after that.

In third grade, our teacher, Miss Smith, read aloud to the class during lunch hour. She was a bespectacled Caucasian woman with a musical voice. She read *Charlotte's Web*, and I was mesmerized, drawing sketches of Wilbur the pig and spider webs at my desk. Miss Smith inspired me to start reading books on my own. Mom and Dad used to read to me as a kid. I later realized borrowing library books was free, which helped our family budget. Reading stories began to fill my days and nights. I borrowed books from the library every week and spent hours in Grandma's mango tree transporting myself to mysterious lands through time, all by the written word.

On Thursdays, Miss Smith handed our class over to Miss

Branson who would teach us square dancing. I absolutely loved doing a "do si do" during the "Virginia Reel." We giggled when we accidentally rammed into each other back to back in the process. In a crazy way, square dancing was a type of storytelling, recalling a time and place in America long past.

When I was about eight, I was given the choice of going to Japanese language school or hula school. I picked hula school because ... why not? My favorite cousin, Kendra, did hula, so why shouldn't I? It was the ultimate storytelling dance. Each hand gesture, body bend, even the wink of an eye told the story of Hawaiian places, gods and heroes. I really got into it, mostly because the implements were colorful or noisy. The *uli uli* (feather shaker) and *pu'ili* (split bamboo) were my favorites and I went all out to *ami* to the left and *u'ehe* with vigor. My teacher, Mrs. Vincent, was a generously proportioned Portuguese/Hawaiian woman who commanded attention. During my first "hula graduation" she gave me the name "Kealoha" which means "The Loved One." I felt so special to receive such a lovely name. I felt glamorous in my fuschia-colored satin *holoku* and, of course, my graduation hula was titled, "Kealoha." Although I regretted not being able to read or speak Japanese with my grandmothers as I grew older, little did I know how hula would dramatically change my future!

CHAPTER 4
POOR, BUT NOT POOR

Although both my parents worked, they probably didn't make much money. I say probably, because I never asked them how much they made as public school teachers in the early Sixties. But from what I can remember, we lived in low-cost, possibly free, housing as part of their compensation. These "teachers' cottages" were wooden boxes in a cluster across the street from Wahiawa General Hospital. Until age four, I remember living in a house with two large rooms with a shower and toilet in between. One side of the house was the kitchen-dining-living room while the other side was the bedroom. The wood floors were painted dark brown and large lauhala leaf mats served as area rugs. The place smelled like mildew.

From age five to eight, we lived in a slightly newer cottage a stone's throw away. This house had roll-out carpeting in the living room and vinyl on the kitchen and bathroom floors. The three bedrooms were tiny. My sister Lisa who was four years younger than me and I shared one room; my parents slept in the other. The third bedroom was so small, we could only fit Dad's desk and our toybox in it. The washing machine sat in the bathroom and emptied into a deep, double concrete sink. Lisa and I took bubble baths in our respective sinks until we were old enough to take showers on our own.

It's fun when you're poor and don't really know it. We went to the library weekly, and Mom read to Lisa and me almost every night. The free library system is truly one of our country's greatest gifts to poor families.

Going to the beach was always a blast. We played there for hours. Dad was the sea monster and growled and chased us around the shallows. He let us jump off his shoulders into the water. I thought he was so strong to do that! Mom always made the yummiest *musubi* (rice balls), which we gobbled down with sliced hot dogs or Vienna sausage cooked in soy sauce. We also ate pickled *daikon* (radishes) which were dyed bright yellow and washed it all down with iced water from a fat thermos. Poor? I didn't think so.

Back then, Wahiawa was still pretty rural. How do I know? Mom raised chickens in the backyard. They were from eggs she hatched in an incubator each spring to show her kindergarten students where chicks come from.

"See that little tooth at the tip of the chick's beak?" Mom pointed out to Lisa and me. "That's to help it peck through its shell." They were so darn fluffy and cute. But when the egg-hatching lesson was over, Mom brought the chicks home to raise them — for eating! Lisa and I watched half in horror, half in awe as Dad calmly tied the chicken's legs together and sliced its artery. I was given the job of dipping the bird into a hot tub of water and plucking it. The wet feathers smelled so bad, I just whined and let Dad finish the job. Then Mom, always the teacher, dressed the chicken, saying things like, "See? Here's the stomach. Can you feel the grain still in there? And here's the gizzard. We can eat it." Yeah, good luck with that! I just refused to eat the fried chicken on my plate that night. After that, Mom took the chickens to her brother's farm instead of keeping them.

Even when we moved out of Wahiawa we lived frugally,

though I didn't realize it. I spent one summer going to sewing class behind a small barber shop. Between haircuts and shaves the shop's owner, Mrs. Koizumi, taught four of us how to draft, cut and stitch our own dresses, shorts and mu'u-mu'us. I took it as a badge of honor if I could sew a shorty-mu'u for less than three dollars — including the cost of a zipper and a spool of thread. I sewed my own dresses all through high school.

As financially modest as we were, I would soon learn what poor really was.

"Let's clean out your closet," suggested Mom one spring day. "There are surely some clothes you no longer wear."

She started pulling dresses I had outgrown in first grade one by one off the lead pipe that served as a closet rack. I pretty much agreed with all the ones she suggested we give away. Except the one with bunches of cherries on it.

"I like that one!" I whined.

"It's too small for you!" said Mom, folding it and putting it into a paper shopping bag.

"No! I like it!" I begged. "Don't give it away!"

Mom would not budge.

"Let's go," she said as she placed the bag in the car with several others filled with bedding and canned goods.

Clueless, I huffed and sat in the back seat with the bags, my cherry dress sitting right on top. Mom drove to a part of Wahiawa where I had never been. She stopped in front of a house with weathered blackish wood walls. There were rusty screens but no glass in the windows. From the backseat of the car, I could see spaces between the rough, splintered wall panels, and it was dark inside the building. No electricity. There were at least four young children playing in the yard, which was just a patch of weeds. A thin, young Hawaiian woman with several missing teeth approached the car as Mom got out.

"Hi Mrs. Leahi (not her real name)," I heard Mom greet

the woman. Mrs. Leahi grinned broadly. Her toothless smile frightened me a little. Mom and Mrs. Leahi chatted. The children carried the paper bags up the sagging wooden steps and through the crooked doorway. I watched as my cherry dress disappeared into the blackness.

"Okay, goodbye!" I heard Mom say. "See you in school!"

I waved shyly, as it dawned on me that some of Mrs. Leahi's children were Mom's students.

"Mrs. Leahi has ten children," Mom said matter-of-factly as she drove away.

A couple days later, I saw my cherry dress at school. It was being worn by a girl named Donna Leahi. I smiled at her and she smiled back. I thought briefly about saying something but decided not to. My mom had given me a lesson in kindness and dignity.

CHAPTER 5
GIFTS OF ALOHA

loha means love in the Hawaiian language. Growing up, I was surrounded by people who gave their aloha generously. Over the years, I realized each encounter, each experience, each shared joke or ghost story was a gift that enriched my life. Each gift built upon the next to guide me to a lifetime of storytelling. I could never repay these people, only pay it forward.

Ukulele Man — Growing up with a sister four years younger in a neighborhood of "teachers' cottages" meant having few other kids to play with. There were a bunch of bachelors and spinsters in the hood. I couldn't even ride my bike because the street in front of our house was full of potholes and loose gravel. So one day, Mom and Dad gave me an ukulele. But who would teach me to play? My parents bundled me off to Dad's sister's home in Kekaha, Kaua'i, one summer. Aunty Hiroko's husband, Charlie, opened a whole new world of music and entertainment for me.

Uncle Charlie Kaneyama had a deeply wrinkled face, sort of like a Shar Pei. He was a slight man with slicked back hair and black horn-rimmed glasses. His day job was working for Kekaha Sugar Company as a historian and eventually, its safety director. But his passion was being an entertainer and musician. Uncle Charlie was the undisputed "Ukulele Man" of Kaua'i. Conservatively, he taught three thousand Kaua'i kids over three generations to play the ukulele, not to mention hundreds of senior citizens.

In the 1940s, he had his own band — Charlie Kaneyama and the Merry Melodiers — that became wildly popular on Kaua'i and Oahu. Besides "Big Band" tunes, the group played "exotic" tropical music made popular by Martin Denny in the 1950s. There was a vibraphone, lots of cymbal brushing, tinkling chimes and a gourd that was stroked with a stiff wire brush. Uncle Charlie hid off stage and made the monkey calls!

He was always laughing and smiling and telling jokes (he had a "million" of them). His idol was Jack Benny. And he made us giggle with delight while grossing out the cousins at the same time by passing gas as he walked by.

"Hey, let me take a look at that," he'd say, bending over to look at a book I was reading. He'd let out a toot and all of us laughed until our stomachs ached.

Each of his five kids (my cousins) played ukulele and other instruments. His son Ray actually played keyboards professionally with Martin Denny! Uncle Charlie had a large room in his house filled with instruments — many of which he taught himself to play — chimes, clarinet, harmonica, xylophone, saxophone, all manner of guitars and even a Chinese gong! I spent hours sampling the instruments or leafing through his alphabetically organized chest of drawers filled with mimeographed lyrics and chords.

"Take whatever you want, just not the original," he said.

Each summer, he packed up a dozen or more cousins, aunts and uncles to caravan to the Kekaha Sugar Company's cabin in Kokee for a vacation. We hiked the mountain trails around Waimea Canyon, picking wild plums and *lilikoi* along the way. One summer, a wild horse chased my Aunty Sally and cousins Glenn, Lois and Michael into a tree. At night, we toasted marshmallows in the fireplace and broke out the instruments. We played a lot of *hapa haole* tunes, songs from musicals and even Japanese classics like *Kojo no Tsuki* with Uncle Charlie playing the melancholy refrain on his clarinet.

As I look back, I realize how much I was learning through music. Playing the ukulele and piano introduced me to chords, melodies and harmonies. The lyrics of the songs were language lessons if they were in Hawaiian or Japanese. *Ka makani* was wind in Hawaiian. *Sakura* means cherry blossom in Japanese. The songs were stories set to music, and I loved a good story. King Kamehameha was the Conqueror of the Islands, and we cried out for Bill Bailey to please come home.

On our way back from Kokee, we often stopped to see my dad's mom in Kekaha. Her name was Akino, but we called her Kaua'i Grandma. She and my unmarried Aunty Yuki lived in the very same house where my dad and his seven siblings grew up. It was a compact, rough-timbered planta-tion house with a metal roof. There was a small living room, three tiny bedrooms and a water closet on the entry floor. The kitchen was down a short flight of stairs. The floor was packed sand and dirt. Against one wall was a galvanized sink and black four burner gas stove. There was a pantry in the corner, a thirties era refrigerator and against the opposite wall was a long wooden picnic table with benches. I don't know how a family of ten could live in this house. Now that I think of it, they never did. Several of my dad's older siblings got married or moved out by the time he was born!

Kaua'i Grandma was like the Buddha statue at Kamakura. She sat on the front porch with her legs folded under her (how did she do that?) and watched us play around the ferns growing through the hard pack sand/soil in the front yard. I never understood her Japanese; mine was limited to "Good Morning" and telling her how old I was by showing her on my fingers. Aunty Sally, who was second youngest in the family before my dad, said in her younger days that Kaua'i

Grandma brought in extra money washing work clothes for the bachelors on the plantation.

"She looked like a witch, stirring the red-dirt-stained pants like a brew in a big metal pot over a wood fire," Aunty Sally laughed. "It wasn't a lot of money, but on the Fourth of July, she had enough to buy us loaves of French bread cut in half and slathered with guava jelly!"

Aunty Sally was so used to this shabby, old plantation house, she didn't mind cleaning our clothes at the outdoor wash basin using a washboard and hanging them to dry. There was an old wringer machine in the corner of the wash area, but Aunty Sally said it was broken. As I look back, it was like living in an under-developed country, except there was indoor plumbing and electricity.

The most traumatic part of staying with Kaua'i Grandma was the outdoor *furo* (soaking tub). It was in a shed against the kitchen wall. Steamy and dark, it was the perfect living quarters for brown spiders the size of my hand! They hung out on the inside of the entry door right before my face.

"Shoo!" Aunty Sally shouted and swatted at them with a towel. This was terrifying because a spider would scurry into a dark corner on the ceiling, and I was deathly afraid it would drop onto my head. Or sometimes, to my horror, she simply said, "Oh, it's harmless, just open the door!"

After washing with soap and rinsing outside the wooden *furo*, I climbed in and s-l-o-w-l-y eased into the hot water. The water came up to my chin as I squatted on the bench. The floor of the tub was galvanized metal, but the rest of the tub was wood. Someone (probably Aunty Yuki) had heated the water earlier using the wood-burning heater outside that supplied the entire house. (I believe Kauai Grandma didn't get an electric water heater until the 1970s.) I later told Dad I was afraid of the spiders in the bath house. Suddenly, it was decided I would go to Uncle Charlie and Aunty Hiroko's house to bathe. What a relief!

Aunty Hiroko was always kind to the "out of town" nieces and nephews. She graciously put up with the annual summer "invasion" of her peaceful home by hordes of Oahu relatives. Sometimes, I arrived on Kaua'i before my other cousins and spent quality time with Aunty Hiroko. She was an awesome baker. She taught me how to cut butter into flour, roll Russian tea cookies, bake a three-layer cake and crimp pie crust. Nothing seemed to kerfuffle her, even when I got the measles and had to stay at her house an extra week. She nursed me back to health with the Japanese version of "chicken soup" — *okai* — rice porridge with just a pinch of salt.

"So sorry about being sick," I murmured from under the thick *futon* quilt.

"Oh, no problem," she laughed gently. "At least you'll never get it again."

Each summer, I came away grateful for what Uncle Charlie and Aunty Hiroko taught me through music, laughter and pies made with care. There are stories in each activity, and all I needed to do was pay attention.

Even ghost stories have a place in Hawai'i. I love the island of Kaua'i because it is the most haunted of the islands. Every one of my relatives there claimed to have encountered a ghost or something supernatural. My favorite story was about Aunty Toyo. She was Dad's eldest sister. She married a wealthy investor. They lived in a large *luna* house — some called it a mansion — in Waimea, about twenty minutes up the road from Kaua'i Grandma's house in Kekaha. One night in November 1949, Kaua'i Grandpa got sick and ended up at Waimea hospital. That evening, Toyo was sitting at her vanity, brushing her hair. A movement caught her eye. She looked up at the bedroom door and saw Grandpa looking at her from the hall.

"*Otoosan* (Father)!" she exclaimed. "What are you doing here?"

He looked at her quite sadly. Just then, the telephone rang.

"Hello?" Toyo answered, mystified.

"Toyo, it's Masao (her oldest brother). Dad just died."

"What? But Dad's right here …" said Toyo. But when she looked at the doorway, he was gone. The family concluded Grandpa's spirit had come to say goodbye to Toyo before his heavenly journey.

Acceptance of spirits and ghosts may seem curious in a family like ours composed mostly of Buddhists and some Christians. But in Hawai'i, they are part of the storytelling tradition. I voraciously consumed myths and folktales wherever I found them. Legends from Hawai'i, Japan, Europe and all manner of Indigenous people told me so much about their history and values. This was storytelling that required me to respect the beliefs of others. In many ways, these stories showed us our commonality and provided another way of "getting along" in the world

As for the Aunty Toyo story, I learned this sort of visitation by the deceased was common among the relatives and within the larger Japanese American community. Sometimes, the loved one visited in the form of a large moth. My mother said she was visited by her mother's spirit that way. And many decades later, my sister and I were visited by moths at different locations when we gathered for our mother's memorial service in 2019. What was I to make of this? I felt a warm gratitude that I was so beloved, that I would be visited by my mother's spirit. *A hui hou.* Until we meet again.

THE PIANO TEACHER — For about five years through tenth grade, I took piano lessons in part because I was a nerdy wallflower with a lot of time on my hands. What a blessing to receive those lessons from a passionate doyenne named Toma Gurney. A real firecracker, this one, she had platinum white hair and wore form-fitting shifts, often with Chinese style collars. She smelled like baby powder and wore glittery cat-eye glasses. I couldn't stop staring at her costume diamond or emerald earrings. The bangles on her wrist rattled every time she played a passage on the keyboard.

What made this former concert pianist decide to teach in podunk Aiea was beyond me. She did say she had injured her hands and so couldn't play professionally. She said she was good friends with Liberace (she called him "Leeb"). I played my darndest for her — Bach, Mozart, Beethoven — and actually got pretty good at it. So much so, that I thought maybe I'd become a piano teacher just like her. She kept telling me that soon I'd be ready for some pop. Confused (and admittedly a little thirsty since I walked to lessons after school) I replied, "Oh, that sounds good!"

I thought, "How nice of her to spend a buck on a Coke for all her students!" There was a drive-in on the floor below that also sold fruit punch and green river drinks.

Was I surprised on the day she got up and announced, "Time for some pop!" She walked to the cupboard across the room and flung open the doors.

"That's a weird place to store a Coke," I thought.

"Here it is!" she declared, walking back to the piano with a music book in her hands. My jaw dropped. A book of popular music! POP! I smiled weakly. "Thanks, Mrs. Gurney. Can't wait." Little did I know this total misunderstanding on my part would lead to astonishing things!

The AHS Majorettes — I cannot recall how a small group of us decided to form a twirling team (we called ourselves by the old-fashioned term: majorettes). It was a short-lived chapter in my life but important in that it pushed me out of my Japanese American comfort zone and exposed me to "Mainland" culture.

Sherri Conn was a couple years older than me. Her sister Debbie was my age along with a mutual friend, Karen Kennedy. In the strange racial order at our public school,

Sherri, Debbie and Karen fell into the category of "military mainland *haole*," so yes, they were from white military families from the Mainland. Another team member was Gail Borrales. She was my neighbor and a "local Portuguese" meaning she was not a "mainland haole" even though her skin was white. In Hawai'i, Portuguese are considered an ethnic group like the Chinese, Japanese and Filipinos because they immigrated to the Islands to work on the plantations, too. The rest of us, Brenda Tome, Shari Uejo, Pam Hayashi, Marjorie Inn and I were Japanese or Chinese American.

Sherri convinced us to take twirling lessons at Pearl Harbor naval base where her family lived. We loved the idea of twirling batons, marching in parades and performing at the football half time, or at least, Sherri did. This twirling thing was foreign to us local gals, but our mainland friends seemed to enjoy sharing their cultural activity with us. We spent an hour or two after school practicing in Gail's garage since her home was right above the high school, a close walk.

We ordered white satin outfits with embroidered "A"s on the front. In that year, we marched two miles in a local parade and won first place, much to the shock of Kailua High School's team, the perennial champions. We also performed at one football half time. One could say our experiment with "mainland culture" was a bit of a bust, but we DID get our photo in the yearbook.

Aiea Swinging Singers — Who would ever name a high school choir the Aiea Swinging Singers (initials ASS)? It turns out they needed a piano accompanist. I heard about it through June Ito, one of Mrs. Gurney's students. June was the current accompanist and a junior at Aiea High.

"Why don't you come and play for the choir?" June asked innocently. "You will get an exception and won't have to take P.E. No showers in the locker room!"

I perked up. No P.E.? Sounded good to me, a high school freshman with absolutely NO physical talent.

"Here's the music. *Chim Chim Cher-ee* from Mary Poppins. Learn it. I'll be your page turner," June said casually. She turned and left.

Was I ever glad Mrs. Gurney had widened my repertoire to include popular music. I practiced that song for hours. When I went in to play for the choir teacher, Mrs. Edwina Siu, I was shocked to see the entire select choir there, too. Welcome to the audition!

"Okay, let's do this," called out Mrs. Siu. June stood by my side, ready to turn pages. Mrs. Siu looked at me. "One two three, one two three …" she counted and I began to play. The whole thing was a blur. I remembered how the fluorescent lights made the music page so bright. The voices were incredibly loud. Was my hair flying backward? June calmly turned the next page, and the next.

"Good!" exclaimed Mrs. Siu at the last chord. "Shall we do it again from the second verse?" Thank goodness I had practiced. I could pick it up from anywhere. We played through the song from the second verse.

When the bell rang, all the choir members got out of their chairs and started shuffling to the doors.

"Practice your parts!" shouted Mrs. Siu. "Practice like Lori did!" She flashed me a smile. "Wow!" I said softly. "I guess I got the position."

June smirked and picked up her books. "Of course, you did." And walked out.

Choir culture at Aiea High School thrust me into a world of discovery and appreciation. Previously, I had been in my own little bubble — a Japanese American middle-class family, two working parents, Japanese American friends, fairly good grades. In the Swinging Singers, it was *Hawai'i 'Ohana* (family) writ large. First off, there were a lot of upperclassmen because this was the *select* choir. Everyone had to audition. And then, because it was a choir, the students could really sing! The GPA of the group — a totally mixed bag from June, who had a 4.0 her entire high school career to the seniors who depended on getting an "A" from Mrs. Siu to graduate. There were students from the projects (Halawa Housing), football players, cheerleaders, students with step mothers and step fathers, students with no fathers, students raising their kids and those who worked part time. The ethnicities were like fried rice. Everything was in there. Chinese, Japanese, Hawaiian, Filipino, Samoan, Portuguese, Mainland *haole* and every blend.

Mrs. Siu had more than an annual spring concert in mind. She was going to transform her select choir into an international performing group. She was ideally suited to the task. Half Chinese, half Puerto Rican with cream-colored skin and a sparkling smile, she grew up surrounded by the music and dances of Polynesia. She graduated from Maryknoll, a Catholic school on Punahou Street and then from the University of Hawai'i. Along the way, she sang and danced the hula with the Royal Hawaiian Band. They performed at the Kapiolani Bandstand and at Aloha Tower when passenger ships like the Lurline came to port. She also performed with Hawaiian singer Danny Kaleikini at the Kahala Hotel, one of Oahu's premier resorts on the "other" side of Diamond Head.

So when the Aiea Swinging Singers took shape, it was all about putting on a Hawaiian show in Waikiki venues. Sure, we would do gigs dressed in our "American" outfits — blazers and ties for the guys, jumpers with pumps for the gals — singing *"Chim Chim Cher-ree."* But our audiences really got fired up for the Polynesian show. That's when I transformed from pianist to ukulele player (Thank you, Uncle Charlie!), singer and Maori poi ball dancer. It was a bonus for me that I learned to make and dance with poi balls in sixth grade for a May Day program. And no wonder the Waikiki hotels loved the show. It had ancient Hawaiian chants, *hapa-Haole* tunes, Samoan slap dancing, Maori *haka* and poi balls and the ever-popular Tahitian dance with the choir members in full plumage pulling hapless audience members on stage to wiggle along! The "band" played ukulele, guitar, bass and all the Tahitian drums.

The performances were excellent job training for a career as a performer. Be on time for transportation to a venue, keep track of the show rundown (Which songs are in? Which are out?), do a quick costume change, wear false eyelashes if you're a female performer, set up, tune and tear down instruments quickly, be ready to fill-in if another dancer or drummer is absent. It's not surprising that several Swinging Singers went on to careers in Polynesian performance including O'Brien Eselu, Lyle Soberano, Carlton Damaso and Sonya Mendez.

Year by year, our performance schedules grew. Freshman year (1971), we took a trip to Kaua'i to perform. My sophomore year (1972), we were touring the Mainland: Disneyland; Hershey, PA; and Milwaukee, WI. Milwaukee?? Apparently, an executive at Milwaukee Insurance Company caught our show in Waikiki and arranged for us to perform at his conference. To get there, we embarked on a year-long fundraising binge, collecting and rolling a ton of newspapers for agriculture packing houses and selling doughnuts and coffee at football games. During the trip, I remember the air in downtown Hershey smelled like chocolate! And in Milwaukee, people in the pubs drank beer from glass boots.

By junior year (1973), we hit the jackpot! Mrs. Siu informed our school principal that the Swinging Singers were going on a two-week tour of Asia! First stop, New Zealand, home of the most beautiful people on earth. I mean, physically beautiful. Previously, I thought nothing could beat the good-looking Hawaiian-Chinese friends I knew in Hawai'i. But I was stunned by the handsomeness of the Maori-British boys and girls we encountered. And their British accents were absolutely adorable. We did most of our performances at night, then toured the country during the day.

At our big concert at Auckland Town Hall, I felt a surge in my heart when our choir gave a full-throated traditional greeting (*Aloha Chant*) followed by our version of *Hana Chant* as the men danced. It was as if the ancient ones of Hawai'i were calling out to the spirits of the indigenous Maori people of New Zealand.

Ha'aheo o Hana la.
Ha'aheo o Hana la.
Ku'u pu'u Kauiki la
Ku'u lei lokelani la
Ke ali'i la
Ka'ahumanu a no Kamehameha
He inoa no Ka'ahumanu a
no Kamehameha

Proud is Hana
Proud is Hana
My hill of Ka'uiki
My rose lei
The chief
Ka'ahumanu and Kamehameha
(Remember) the names of
Ka'ahumanu and Kamehameha

We were nervous performing the Maori portion of our program in Auckland. Would the New Zealanders scoff at our interpretation of Maori singing and dancing? When our girls stepped onstage with our beaded skirts clacking and swinging, the crowd roared. They cheered through the entire dance and clapped when the poi balls started turning like hummingbird wings. We were so relieved!

During the day, we visited the hot springs of Rotorua and marveled at the incandescent pinpoints above us as our skiffs silently glided inside the Waitomo Glowworm Caves. But a true cultural encounter would become our highlight.

We were the guests of a Maori tribe. They invited us to their *marae*, or meeting complex where we were welcomed in the Maori language and invited for tea in their *wharenui*, or large building. I knew this was special and took my cues from Mrs. Siu, who sat with the rest of us on the floor and politely listened to the speech-making. Some of the tribe's women stood and performed a dance. In return, our male students performed *Kamate*, a loud and fierce Maori *haka* — or challenge dance — a display of strength and unity. I was melting under the gaze of the Maori elders — stern and at the same time, benevolent. They told us: "Young people who are grounded in culture are the hope for indigenous people." I only had the tiniest understanding of the struggle of indigenous people. I knew Native Hawaiians were historically mistreated by European and American capitalists. It dawned on me that the Maori people experienced the same oppression. This was an education I would have never received in a classroom back home.

The stops in Australia and the Philippines were so short, they became a blur. I recall petting a koala while visiting a sanctuary in Melbourne and performing at the officer's club at Subic Bay Naval Station in the Philippines. While at Subic, I visited briefly with an aunt and uncle on my mother's side. Uncle Chang was the catering manager at the base. I remember drinking coconut water from a green coconut and dining on delicious garlic butter prawns ten inches long. They don't fool around in the Philippines!

We ended our tour doing a five-night gig at the Keio Plaza Hotel in Tokyo. This was literally "sing for your supper" time. Each night, we packed the ballroom for the Japanese version of "Luau Time." This was my first trip to Japan, the home of my grandparents. I kept thinking, "I look like you. My name is Japanese. But I am from Hawai'i!" Each time an audience member looked at me, I felt they were checking out an oddity, like a puppy in the pet store window.

Mom's voice from my youth came flooding back. Mostly her frustration with how Japanese from Japan, even her own relatives, looked down on Japanese in Hawai'i.

"They think we're all low class," she fumed. It was as if those who left the Motherland were losers and quickly forgotten. To Mom, this schism was nearly unbearable. In Hawai'i, her immigrant parents became wealthy, well-respected dairy farmers and businesspeople. They owned real estate, a fleet of delivery trucks and were the first in their neighborhood to own a Model T. During World War II, they bought war bonds and their names appeared in the local newspaper. But when a few relatives visited Honolulu, they took a free tour in my parents' car, gobbled down the rice balls Mom made for them and left without expressing any thanks. Curiously, my father's relatives from Japan never visited but welcomed visits by my cousin who was doing genealogy research. The bottom line for me growing up was Japanese from Japan don't appreciate those in Hawai'i.

As I looked at the Japanese audience, I saw really pale people who were enjoying a show without any appreciation for the Japanese Americans performing in it. There was no knowledge of our history or accomplishments. No love. How strange for me to be one of them, but not.

On the night of our last performance, several dancers had tears rolling down their cheeks as they did their hula. They thought they would never be back. I stayed dry-eyed the whole time. I would be back, I vowed, with a better understanding of my ambivalence.

Be Gifted — George B. Carter believed in young people who may not have believed in themselves. A retired Air Force major who ran an Asian import shop in Aiea, Mr. Carter was the quintessential Mainland *haole*: blue eyes, silvery hair and very white. His son and I were classmates, so I easily accepted an invitation to come to a meeting of "gifted" youth called Serteens. It was a project of the Sertoma Club, which stood for "Service to Mankind." It was George Carter's ambition to build up a generation of young, local leaders by matching them with business and government mentors. He used his military contacts to arrange for a group retreat at Kilauea Military Camp on Hawai'i Island that became an annual tradition. Hiking Kilauea volcano was required. More than anything, Mr. Carter wanted us to "bust out" of our provincial "local kid" myopia and "be gifted." His favorite phrase was: "May I slay a dragon for you?"

So it was truly an honor that the Honolulu Sertoma Club sent me and Darryl Ching, a student from Kalani High School, to the Gifted Students Foundation retreat in Sandusky, Ohio. For three summer weeks in 1972, we joined dozens of other "gifted students" from across the country to study economics, history and art in a college setting. We traveled to Valley Forge, West Point, New York City and Washington D.C.

While in the nation's capital, Darryl and I lunched with Hawai'i Congresswoman Patsy Takemoto Mink. I was so tongue-tied sitting across a political legend! Congresswoman Mink was the first Asian American woman and first woman of color elected to Congress. She championed civil rights and education and co-authored Title IX of the Education Amendments of 1972, which created opportunities for women in athletics. (It was later renamed the Patsy T. Mink Equal Opportunity in Education Act in 2002.) I picked at my plate of rigatoni. "Why didn't I prepare some thoughtful questions for this lunch?" I agonized. "What a lunkhead I am!" I'm sure the congresswoman didn't consider me very gifted, but she was gracious and suggested that Darryl and I try the spumoni ice cream. Lesson learned: be prepared! (Darryl would eventually graduate from West Point Military Academy, which we visited that summer. Congresswoman

Mink posthumously received the Presidential Medal of Freedom from President Barack Obama on November 24, 2014.)

At this student retreat, many of the things I learned were serendipitous. I even learned that word — serendipitous — while I was in Sandusky. I learned how to macrame. I learned about Jewish traditions from fellow students who told me I was a *goy* and "*Oy vey*! Have you never met a Jew before?" (I hadn't.) I lay in the grass at dusk and watched fireflies for the first time in my life. I played the harmonica and rode the biggest roller coasters I'd even seen at Cedar Point. I marveled at this version of America. If George Carter wanted a "bust out" year for me, this was pretty much it.

Speech Club — Ninth and tenth grades were fraught with insecurity and despair. I had braces, glasses and knock knees. Zits, yes, and a fragile group of friends from intermediate school who perhaps took pity on me and let me tag along with them at Aiea High School. Remember how I became the choir accompanist because I had a "lot of time" to practice the piano? Well, I had a "lot of time" on Saturdays and Sundays, too. I joined the Speech Club because a classmate told me, you can meet friends and get over your shyness. The Club competed in speech contests on Saturdays around the Island. So there was another lonely day I could fill with some good old-fashioned speechmaking!

I considered the options — debate, extemporaneous speaking and storytelling. Wait! What? Storytelling was a competitive category? Unbeknownst to my fellow club members, as a child I used to love making up stories in my head and telling them outloud to nobody in particular. This often led to my mom yelling out the kitchen window, "Stop talking to yourself! People will think you're crazy!"

So in a wild turn of events, and to my mother's horror, I began competing in speech contests in the storytelling category. And I was good. My winning stories were "Tikki Tikki

Tembo" retold by Arlene Mosel and "Three Strong Women: A Tall Tale from Japan" by Claus Stamm.

Storytelling is a mixture of speaking and acting and character-voices and emotions rolled into three minutes. It demands eye contact, reading an audience and eliciting laughter or applause and pretending this is the first time you've ever shared this tale, so fresh is its telling! This was, again, another building block in being a storyteller and journalist, though I didn't even know it.

CHAPTER 6
ASSAULT WITH SEXUAL INTENT

The problem with being a female assault victim is you find yourself questioning yourself over something that is NOT YOUR FAULT. But over the years, I kept wondering: Could I have prevented becoming a victim? Should I have taken that short-cut along a road lined with homes rather than staying on Aiea Heights Drive, choked by exhaust-spewing traffic? Was it my outfit?

I was a high school sophomore walking to my piano lesson from Aiea High School. To avoid the noisy and scary-fast traffic along Aiea Heights Drive, I took a stroll down a side street lined with homes, with very little traffic. I had never heard of anything "bad" happening in my hometown, much less in the neighborhood near my high school. In fact, this little side street was always deserted when I walked through, except for … that one day.

I walked looking down at my feet. I didn't want to stumble on a pothole. I was a gangly tenth grader with hair cut way too short. I was wearing a cheap rayon outfit — red blouse and flared skirt with white polka dots and baggy black tights. No Vogue cover, for sure. As I approached the intersection where I would turn left to rejoin busy Aiea Heights

Drive, a round Polynesian man in a white T-shirt, jeans and sunglasses hurriedly walked toward me. I looked up, startled, but relaxed when he kept going straight. But in an instant, I heard rapid footsteps behind me and the man grabbed my right arm. The piano books I'd been clutching to my chest flew onto the street and my shoulder bag hit the ground.

"Don't yell. I've got a gun," he growled and started dragging me back toward one of the houses.

"No!" I squeaked. I couldn't yell, I was so shocked and frightened. I planted my right foot and tried to pull loose. "No!"

I looked around in a panic. There wasn't anyone around to hear me even if I did scream. Later, I was told by police that there was another man waiting and watching from a nearby carport. He obviously knew the man who was now dragging me along the asphalt. I was crying now, dreading what was going to happen next — when a miracle happened.

A young man and a female passenger drove next to us and STOPPED at the intersection. The driver leaned out of his window and shouted, "Hey, are you alright?" I was panic-stricken.

"No, no!" I was still squeaking. "Help!" In my mind I was telling myself, "Scream, stupid, scream! He doesn't know this is a problem! Please, Mister, can't you see the piano books on the road? He's dragging me!"

"No problem," the round man yelled cheerily. "She's my girlfriend!"

I looked at the driver and shook my head in a panic.

"No, I'm not!" I tried to pull away again.

"Let her go!" yelled the driver. He was getting out of his car.

The round man abruptly let go and scurried away.

The next hour or so was a blur. I remember the woman in the car encouraging me to get in and wait with her. The driver, who turned out to be her husband, walked a block across the street to a gas station pay phone and called police. I mean, that's how close we were to a very busy street with potentially scores of witnesses! Someone had called my dad, who began driving to Aiea from downtown. Mom hadn't gotten home from the school where she taught yet. Meanwhile, two police officers put me in the back of their squad car and drove around the neighborhood to see if I could "spot the guy." Of course, we never found him. They asked me if the suspect was Hawaiian or Samoan.

"What kind of question is that?" I thought incredulously. "I don't know," I murmured.

It turns out the man who rescued me was a soldier at a base nearby. My father, then a major in the Army Reserve, wrote a glowing letter of thanks to the soldier's commanding officer. Every time I re-live this scary time in my mind, I thank God for putting that soldier and his wife right there, right then. But I also feel a simmering rage. I know this experience has skewed my attitude toward sex. "Men just want to have sex. Rape people. They are animals." I never sought counseling for this trauma. Like a "good Japanese girl" I kept it to myself because of *haji* — the shame it would bring to me and my family. Maybe it was my fault. Should I have walked a different route? Why didn't I scream louder and put up a fight? Now I know it was not my fault that I became a victim. As I got older, I went on dates but never had a serious boyfriend because I knew what was coming — a sex act, wanted or not. Only after positive relationships with kind and gentle men over several years did I feel safe enough to enjoy lovemaking. Today, I applaud women who have the courage to call out the brutes still among us. These women reject being called a victim. They are survivors. Brava.

CHAPTER 7
MISS TEENAGE AMERICA
— IT LASTS JUST A YEAR

By my junior year in high school, I knew I wanted to go to college and that it would require money which we really didn't have. My parents were public school teachers and they had three daughters to raise. A friend of mine told me about a contest. It was called the Miss Teenage America contest. "The winner gets a $10,000 scholarship," he enthused. "And the best part is there's no swimsuit competition, so you might have a chance!" Ouch.

As it turned out, the local pageant was pretty low-key. Applicants took a current events test, performed a talent (I played Bach on the piano. Again, those lessons were paying off!) and did a live interview with the judges.

I had never entered such a contest before. I later learned that there's an entire "pageant culture" where young women enter several contests over their lifetime to win titles like "Cherry Blossom Queen," "Narcissus Queen" and of course, Miss Hawai'i/Miss America. Some pageant veterans told me later that as a first-time contestant I was definitely at a disadvantage, but others disagreed. The naivete of a novice, they mused, could work in my favor.

Little did I comprehend at the time that all my "I had a lot of extra time" activities would combine into a perfect storm of good fortune. Everything I did because I was the outcast ugly duckling of the class proved to be a benefit. The piano lessons led to accompanying the Aiea Swinging Singers. Accompanying the Swinging Singers led to performances before large audiences in Waikiki, putting on fake eyelashes with ease and surviving a grueling travel itinerary overseas. Joining the speech club to compete in storytelling taught me to look judges straight in the eye and compel them to form a bond with me. And those hours alone reading books and newspapers, encyclopedias and Time-Life books? They filled my head with so much minutiae, I couldn't wait to step out and see the world beyond my island home.

I don't remember much about the program where I was named Miss Teenage Honolulu. The contestants were named by city, rather than state, since each candidate was sponsored by a Dr Pepper bottler and some states had more than one bottler. I was just thrilled to be sharing the spotlight with the "HiBoard" from Liberty House, the department store that staged the show. Liberty House was the Nordstrom of Honolulu back then, and the HiBoard members were those gorgeous high-schoolers selected by the store to model all the latest fashions and be the store's ambassadors." Wow," I thought as I watched the fashion show from off-stage. "Could I ever date a guy that handsome? Could I ever have hair as long and silky as hers?"

A HiBoard member might have tipped me off that I had won the title. With all the contestants standing there, he draped a red carnation lei that went down to my knees around my neck. We all looked at each other. What the ...? The emcee read my name. Awkward, but okay.

The hard work began. We had a couple months to prepare for the national contest in Fort Worth, Texas. John Campbell of Liberty House, who handled community outreach and the HiBoard, focused on the task at hand ... and it was a biggie.

How to take this gal in a homemade shorty mu'umu'u and make her fashion forward enough to represent Hawai'i in a national contest to be broadcast live on CBS? The answer glided into our meeting with a smile. Ellie.

Eleanor McDaniel was a model who worked runways for fashion houses in L.A. in her youth, married young and had a son, got divorced and married an L.A. radio personality (Earl "The Pearl" McDaniel) who became general manager at Honolulu's top radio station, KGMB soon to be KSSK. Blonde and tall with bluer than blue eyes, she still modeled for Liberty House and other fashion brands throughout Honolulu.

"Call me Ellie," she beamed. John Campbell smiled. "I'll leave you two alone," and he walked out of the small meeting room.

The next few weeks were like bootcamp. Ellie was the drill instructor, albeit a diplomatic one. She taught me how to walk (shoulders back, one foot in front of the other), how to sit (ankles crossed, knees together, tougher than it looks), how to do a "turn" if you're working a runway (an Ellie specialty) and yes, "Let's please get some outfits for the upcoming interviews and appropriate shoes."

There was a makeup class (where I learned to use a lip brush at ALL times); I got a stylish comb out for the publicity shoot; someone said I ought to take fresh pineapples to all the other contestants as my "Gift of Aloha" (who thinks up these things?). Ellie and I went up to the Liberty House restaurant for lunch. I thought I'd pass this one with ease, but nope. First of all, she said, watch your calories. No oil, just vinegar, on your salad. Don't butter your entire dinner roll. Break off a small piece, butter it and put that in your mouth. In fact, better yet, don't even eat rolls or butter. No elbows or even forearms on the table. Keep the non-utensil-using hand on your lap. Use your right hand to insert your spoon into the lemon slice and use your left hand to cover and squeeze the lemon into your iced tea. And speaking of spoons, scoop your soup away from yourself and never tip the bowl to get the last drops.

Somewhere in the middle of preparations, someone suggested changing my talent from playing the piano to "something more Hawaiian" like a hula, so I'd be different from the other contestants. Hula!

I called a half dozen members of the Swinging Singers together after school to come up with the music. We gathered at Carlton Damaso's house because his dad had a super-deluxe reel to reel recorder. We recorded a Maori poi ball medley (*Na Waka*, *Manu Rere* and *Hoki Hoki*) making sure it lasted no more than two minutes. We figured, if it was good enough for Waikiki, it was good enough for the Miss Teenage America pageant. There was no question that Ellie was going to be my chaperone. Mom and Dad didn't even plan on going to Fort Worth for the week, much less the pageant itself. We all thought, "It's so far and what are the chances that Hawai'i's first-ever entry — a Japanese American — would even win this thing? We're talking Miss Teenage AMERICA!"

"I'm just looking at this as a great experience," I told Ellie cheerily. "I've never been to Texas. That alone will be fun." So off we flew, cases of pineapples in tow, with absolutely no expectation of winning.

Stepping out of the limousine in front of the hotel in Fort Worth was a thrill. "Welcome Miss Teenage America Contestants," shouted the marquis. Ellie and I shared a tiny corner room she said was "so small you couldn't change your mind in it." We started distributing the pineapples to the other contestants. Most were delighted and found them exotic Others, like Miss Teenage Puerto Rico Evelyn Bonano, thought it was pretty hilarious!

The exciting part of the week for me was preparing for the national broadcast. We got to sing and dance with our host, Ken Berry, the star of the television series "F-Troop." We were doing our Broadway turn as the chorus line for a bona fide entertainer! What a hard worker Ken was. He had an hour or so to learn the lyrics and dance routines prepared by producer Judith Houghton, a no-nonsense redhead with scores of musicals and cruise-ship shows under her trim belt. The opening number was a modified version of "Me and My Gal" which Judy had changed to "Me and My Gals." The opening line went "The bells are ringing, for me and my gals …" The music segued into another tune "Ring Them Bells" which allowed us to ring our bell bracelets and do a full-on kick line like we were at Radio City Music Hall. (To this day, fellow contestants I've kept in touch with and I giggle and sing "Ring Them Bells" as we reminisce about the broadcast!)

Remember this was not a beauty pageant. So we all took our scholastic test and did our interviews with the judges without a swimsuit in sight. These interviews were meant to assess our expression, "poise and appearance." Ellie called it "poison appearance" to get some laughs out of me. They called the talent portion "individual accomplishment," and boy, were these gals talented! Miss Teenage Memphis, Shelia (sp) Ann Peace, sang a dynamite arrangement of "Cabaret" wearing a red satin dress. Miss Teenage Aurora (IL) Paula Zahn (who would go on to become a CNN anchor) played "Gypsies, Tramps and Thieves" on her cello. Miss Teenage San Diego Patti Larkin absolutely slayed us with her twirling routine, tossing that baton to the top of the stage curtains. And Miss Teenage Broken Arrow (OK) Janie Kaye Bowles, who I still write to, got laryngitis and had to switch to playing "Raindrops Keep Falling on My Head" on the piano. I was glad I had switched to Maori poi balls earlier, because yes, no one else was doing them.

And there was such amazing diversity back then in 1973. Shelia and three other contestants were African American; Miss Teenage Atlanta Toyce Ken and I were Asian Americans; and Miss Teenage Puerto Rico was a beaming Latina. (For some reason, the press photographers always grouped Miss Teenage Puerto Rico Evelyn Bonano, Miss Teenage Anchorage Tam Agosti and me together. I guess we were the "exotic places" candidates!)

Wouldn't you know it? I must have been feeling a little stressed because on the night before my interview with the judges, I got the biggest, reddest pimple on my chin! Red as a cherry and in my mind almost as large as one. Ellie swooped into action, applying a hot towel and Clearasil cream, assuring me she had makeup that would cover it. I crawled into bed hoping for a miracle and immediately forgot about it.

On the night of the telecast, I was excited but not at all nervous. Like at the numerous gigs I did with the Swinging Singers in Waikiki, it was all a matter of putting on the eyelashes, arranging the costumes in order and following the rundown. Opening number? Check. Name and hometown? Check. Conversation with Ken Berry (about Maori poi balls, of course). Check. Do an unscripted schtick with a ventriloquist and dummy? Check! And then the worst thing that could happen ... happened. After a week of flawless rehearsals, at the end of my poi ball dance, the balls in my left hand hit each other and collapsed. I untangled them, thinking, "Oh God, please don't be in a knot!" I finally got them going again and completed the dance. Smile, smile, smile. Walk off the stage. Man, I was mad. Not a single error until I was on LIVE television in front of millions of viewers!

"Hey," said Miss Teenage San Diego, Patti Larkin, as she gave me a hug. "I dropped my baton tonight — but the audience was rooting for me. They were sure rooting for you. I guess we just have to move on!" I nodded and reminded myself I wasn't going to win anyway.

The program flew by. Once in a while, I got a peek at the audience. With all the stage lights, I couldn't see Ellie but I knew she was out there. It wasn't until I watched a replay of the program back home in Hawai'i that I realized all the semifinalists' parents were sitting in that audience, except mine. As each finalist finished her performance or interview, the cameras cut to the teen's excited parents applauding or cheering. When I was on stage, the cameras went to Ellie, all sparkly and beaming with a blonde up-do and a mink off her shoulders. "Mrs. Eleanor McDaniel, Chaperone" it said under her image. It was hilarious and endearing. Remember, we weren't going to win.

So it came to this: Ken Berry was ready to announce the name of Miss Teenage America 1974. There were two of us left on stage. Janet Daines, Miss Teenage Logan (UT) and me. On the video replay, I watched my expression as the following thoughts raced through my head. "When he announces me as the first runner up, I am going to jump up and give Janet a big hug and I'll be escorted off the stage. Check."

"Our first alternate is ..." Ken Berry's voice paused, "...Miss Janet Daines from Logan Utah. Ladies and gentlemen, Miss Teenage America 1974 from Honolulu, Hawai'i, Lori Lei Matsukawa!"

The drop-jaw, buggy eyed photo would grace newspapers across the country. I was truly astonished! "Oh quick, what am I supposed to do now?" ran through my mind. "Just like rehearsal," I told myself. "Head stage right, pause, smile smile smile. Head stage left, pause, smile smile smile. Up the middle. Flash a grin to my gal pals all standing back there in rows." The colored streamers dropped from the stage ceiling. The contestants rushed up and its pandemonium, all arms and hugs and "I'm so happy for yous." Unbeknownst to me, Ellie quietly left the auditorium and returned to our teeny corner room to pack our bags. We had to be in New York the next morning.

My senior year in high school was split between being an ordinary student and being Miss Teenage America 1974. When I was home, I attended classes, washed the dishes and did homework like everyone else. Then for two weeks a month, I traveled the country to represent America's young people and promote our main sponsor, the Dr Pepper Company. One of the perks of being Miss Teenage America was getting ten cases of Dr Pepper each month. Each month! My friends and our house guests got used to drinking a lot of Dr Pepper that year. It's actually delicious warm with a slice of lemon in the winter time, and you can cook with it, too.

Miss Teenage America's "job" is to make personal appearances and give speeches (which I wrote myself) at county fairs, school assemblies, banquets, ribbon cuttings at bottling plants (remember, our main sponsor was a soft drink company) and ride the Dr Pepper float in parades at big events like the Orange Bowl, Kentucky Derby and Indianapolis 500. We went to big cities like New York, Los Angeles, Miami, Dallas, Washington D.C. and even overseas to Japan and Peru. But we also visited small towns like Scottsbluff, Nebraska; Tullahoma, Tennessee; and Oil Trough, Arkansas.

I say "we" because I always traveled with a chaperone. It was often my mother but she was a public school teacher so summer was when she could travel the most. Of course, Ellie was a very capable chaperone, but she had a husband and modeling gigs to juggle. So I enlisted my cousin, Diane Morisato, a student advisor at the University of Hawai'i, to chaperone as well. Between the three of them, they logged tens of thousands of miles and countless unpaid hours in a year. Ellie called the chaperone "the woman behind the potted palm" — always close to Lori but unnoticed by all. Mom, Ellie or Diane were responsible for getting me on the plane on time, checking into the hotel, connecting with the event sponsors and making sure I was at the television studio, luncheon, auditorium or reception on time well rested, dressed appropriately and with prepared remarks if necessary. The chaperone was the coat holder, autograph card distributor, the lunch monitor, speech critiquer and bodyguard.

Every trip was an adventure. Riding in the middle of the feathery petals of the Dr Pepper float in the Gasparilla Parade in Tampa made me smile because the pirate-themed parade route was crawling with, you guessed it, PIRATES! I had my first taste of garbanzo bean soup in Miami's Little Havana before the Orange Bowl Parade. Hearing everyone around me speaking Spanish made me appreciate the diversity of the city. At the Indianapolis 500, I rode one of the pace cars around the track. I never knew so many people watched the race from the infield, which some called "the pit." Ahead of the race, I was asked to join the gaggle of "celebrities" who were available for press interviews. That's where I took a picture with Fess Parker, an actor who played Daniel Boone in a television series. No surprise, all the reporters wanted to talk to him, not me! I learned a lot at the Kentucky Derby. Ellie taught me how to place a bet on a horse, even though I was technically not old enough. We picked Cannonade, the favorite, who ended up winning the race. Before the main race, we attended one of those luncheon "mixers" with other celebrities. This time, I was really excited to meet Micky Dolenz of the rock group, The Monkees, Colonel Sanders in his snappy white suit and actor Richard Thomas, best known for his role as John-Boy Walton from the television series "The Waltons." Even Ellie got a charge meeting Heywood Hale Broun, the legendary CBS sports commentator.

When I traveled with Diane, it was like being with the older sister I never had. We went shopping between appearances. Unlike Ellie, she let me eat chocolate and salads with vinegar AND oil. She knew a lot of people at colleges and universities because of her work at the University of Hawai'i. She was always calling on friends to give us tours of their campus to help me decide where I might apply once I graduated. The tours usually ended up with some local cooking somewhere fun. And when we experienced strange or eccentric people on tour, we'd laugh uproariously about them that night in our jammies.

One afternoon between appearances, Diane and I decided to have a creme de menthe sundae at the Beverly Hills Hotel in L.A.

"You know, people in Hollywood are so fake," I commented. "Everyone wants to be famous. Look at that man over there in the corner. He's all dressed up and thinks he looks like Groucho Marx."

Diane grinned and looked over her shoulder. She turned back to me. Her smile had vanished. "That IS Groucho Marx!" she hissed.

I ENCOUNTERED SO many celebrities that year. And although she'll never know it, I learned a lot after meeting Cher during an appearance on the "Sonny and Cher Show." You would think that Cher would be too busy to personally meet with a no-name teenager appearing on the show with her, Sonny and a slew of famous celebrities. But she did!

"Come on in, sweetheart" she called out. She was in the makeup chair in a sequined outfit and Cleopatra-like headdress. I told her what a thrill it was to meet her, oh and I can't wait to do our little schtick that involves us putting down Sonny so he can do a burn into the camera.

"Where're you from?" she asked. I told her Hawai'i, and she said how much she enjoyed visiting the Islands.

The stage manager called us to the set. We taped our act and it was over, just like that! But I will never forget how a mega star like Cher took the time to make a small-town girl feel like the most important person in the room, even for just a couple minutes. I vowed that I would be like Cher, treating everyone with respect and kindness.

As I attended galas and big events, meeting actors, journalists, mayors and CEOs, I pondered what it meant to be a "celebrity," if only for a year. I told myself I'd better enjoy having the Miss Teenage America staff (Carole Wright, Judith Houghton and Charles Meeker, Jr.) planning a year of once-in-a-lifetime experiences and overnight stays at top-of-the-line hotels. I'd better savor riding first class on Braniff Airlines where I first tasted fennel. I'd better appreciate seeing Niagara Falls and dining on a lobster thermidor as long as my forearm. I never wrote so many thank you notes in my life but did so with a grateful heart, because I knew it would last just a year. At a large Dr Pepper banquet where all the men wore tuxedos, I found myself seated beside W. W. Clements, the CEO of the soft drink company. My head began to spin thinking about all the bottlers, advertisers and sales staff I'd met all across the country and how I'm sitting next to the man who controlled their lives. Talk about feeling small! I wasn't expecting another important lesson when I blurted out to Mr. Clements, "I'm really overwhelmed being surrounded by all these important people." He smiled kindly and said in a gentle Texas drawl, "They're all just people, Lori. They all put their pants on one leg at a time."

NOTHING MAKES you feel more American than being Miss Teenage America in another country. For months, I traveled to a lot of states and locales and never got hassled about being Japanese American until … I went to Japan!

I was in a town an hour north of Tokyo called Tone (toh' nay) to open a new Dr Pepper bottling plant. It was the first time Dr Pepper would be bottled and sold in Japan outside a U.S. military base. There were billboards along the highway announcing the arrival of "Daku tah Pep pah." The advance team had me wear a body sash with my name in Japanese characters (*katakana*). At the bottling plant, there was the cere-monial ribbon cutting and photos with the workers in their snazzy jumpsuits and safety helmets. I felt a bit embarrassed because I was taller than many of the men and I'm only five foot three. Photos, handshakes and then off to a supermarket parking lot where they set up a low stage surrounded by cases of "Daku tah Pep pah".

The store manager introduced me to some curious shoppers who really just wanted to taste the free samples. "Missu Teen-ay-ju Amerikaa!" That was my cue. I stepped up onto the plywood stage and waved. Two young boys in the front row gawked and I caught a couple of their words saying in effect, "What?? She's not American!" The manager laughed nervously and admonished them. He then turned to me apologetically and said, "They said you can't be Miss Teenage America because you don't have blonde hair and blue eyes."

"Well!" I thought. "I'll show them!" And I blurted out a few lines in Japanese that I had memorized explaining how I was born in Hawai'i, which is part of the United States.

"Watashi wa Hawai de umaremashita!"

The boys' eyes got big and they looked at each other, aghast! *"Nani?!* (What did she say?)" one of them said, wrinkling his nose and squinting his eyes. I smiled sweetly. "With that accent, now you KNOW I'm American!"

The next day, there was a radio interview planned in Tokyo. The Top-40 DJ could understand a little English and asked if I spoke Japanese. It was the first time I used what would become my stock answer. I use it to this day.

"I am from Hawai'i. When I was a girl, I did not go to Japanese school. I went to hula dance school. So unfortunately, I don't speak Japanese."

"Hu-ra dansu skoo-ru!" exclaimed the DJ delightedly. It turned what could've been a cultural shaming into a cultural *sharing.* He spun John Denver singing "Sunshine on my Shoulders" and we parted as friends.

The Dr Pepper company wasn't done yet. They had planned a photo shoot with me in a silk kimono for their annual Miss Teenage America calendar. It took an hour for the women in the kimono salon to wrap me in layers of silk and a stiff sash around my torso. So much for deep breaths. They put my hair up and inserted floral hair pins. I felt like the empress.

We walked to the cherry trees all in full bloom. Mom said I walked like a boy. "Take smaller steps!" she implored.

The tight kimono and stacked slippers forced me to take tiny shuffle steps. "I'm not getting anywhere!" I grunted.

When it was all said and done, I bowed to the dressers. I hoped I had honored their skill and the beauty of the kimono. Very pretty, they replied. My heart fluttered. For a brief moment, I felt a kinship to these women and the land of my ancestors. Did they look beyond my American-ness and see a Japanese sister? Kimono, cherry blossoms, a dream come true, check!

CHAPTER 8
HEADING TO "THE FARM"

t wasn't my idea to apply to Stanford. Maybe it was my dad's. At the time, I was still thinking of majoring in music to become a piano teacher. I applied to Oberlin and Julliard (stretch schools) and to Northwestern because that's what my senior class counselor suggested. As I read the Stanford brochure, I began to consider my options. It had a Communication Department as well as a Music Department. If I found the music requirements too challenging, I could fall back on communication. During my year as Miss Teenage America, I was interviewed by journalists all the time — at big events like the Indy 500 and small events like county fairs. Get paid to go places and talk to people? I could do that!

The Stanford essay question asked about an event the previous year that deeply affected me or something to that effect. For all the glorious things that happened, I chose to write about a young teen neighbor who died by suicide. Her parents had recently divorced, and she believed it was somehow her fault. I had just returned from a trip that included a visit to St. Jude Children's Hospital in Memphis. As I toured the wards, I saw room after room of very sick children and their parents. Each child was battling a frightening disease. Some had very little hair or none at all. Most were pierced by IVs, breathing tubes or wires. Each young person was struggling mightily. They wanted to live. Their parents wanted them to live. The entire hospital was pushing them to live. And then, I came home to hear about my neighbor. She had life but her personal darkness made her forfeit it. How I wish I could have talked to her about what I saw in Memphis. Life is worth fighting for.

When I got the "thick" envelope telling me I had been accepted to Stanford, I was overjoyed but worried. I was under contract until the new Miss Teenage America was selected in November, and classes at Stanford started in September. Would they reject me if I had to start a quarter late? I wrote to the registrar, Fred Hargaddon, and explained my plight. "Not to worry" he wrote back. I was relieved and only later realized that it is common for Stanford students to get all sorts of breaks just because they had been accepted in the first place. I was getting an inkling of what the word "privilege" meant. No complaints here. After all, the title was what gave me the scholarship to help my parents afford my education. As it was, they still had to take out a second mortgage on the house.

Alumni affectionately call Stanford University "The Farm" because it was established on the stock farm of founders Leland and Jane Stanford. My mom's childhood friend, "Aunty" Ah Heong, and her husband "Uncle" Manny lived close to Stanford, so they offered to pick me up at the airport, drop me off on campus and take me in on Thanksgiving or to Chinatown to eat dim sum and chicken feet on weekends. Uncle Manny dropped me off at the curb outside Branner Hall and wished me well.

I timidly went up the side stairs and knocked on the RA's door. "What in the world is an RA?" I asked myself. (It's resident adviser, Lori.) Andy Hsi opened the door.

"Hi, I'm Lori," I began.

"Hey, welcome! Let me get you to your room!" With a flip of his ponytail, he went into his room and came back with my room key.

"Your roommates are Kathy and Susan. They're nice," he said as we trundled down the hall. He opened the door to my room.

"Yeah, it's a two-room, three-person set up," he continued almost apologetically.

For the next three days, I rattled around the empty dorm pretty much alone. Andy was in and out a lot. I registered for classes and put my sheets on the only un-sheeted bunk (the top one). I looked at the clothes and knickknacks my two roomies had left behind during Christmas break. Lots of plaid flannel shirts and strangely, lots of cashmere sweaters. One very expensive bike.

When you start a quarter late, there's no "Welcome Freshmen!" banner, no Stanford Band concert, no ice cream social or ice breaker games. I was plopped into a strange place where I knew no one. To this day, when I'm stressed, I have nightmares of wandering the Stanford campus looking for my dorm room.

As other students slowly drifted into Branner Hall, I felt a gnawing feeling of inadequacy. A dorm mate named Rob sat at the grand piano in the living room and began playing Beethoven — without music and without mistakes! He heard me playing some Bach earlier and played it back from memory — almost perfectly — because "that was a cool progression." I never played the piano at Stanford after that.

Other students lounged in the dining room, chatting about the medical research they had done during Christmas break. Still others gushed about how much fun they had at Club Med. ("What is Club Med?" I wondered. Back then, there was no way to Google a quick answer.) I was definitely out of my league, intellectually and socio-economically.

As charming as my two roommates were, I still felt a great

divide. Susan was the one with the expensive bicycle. Her father was a Chicago banker, her mother a buyer for Bonwit Teller department store. They were divorced and each had remarried. Her mother sent her a different colored cashmere sweater every month, but Susan simply stuffed them into the closet, preferring to wear plaid flannel shirts. On any given Friday, she could receive a call from her father inviting her to go skiing with him at Aspen or Vail. She and her friends had Piaget wrist watches. ("What is Piaget?" I had never heard of it).

My other roomie, Kathy, was a Georgia peach. A drama major, she loved to hang out at Tresidder Union or other coffee joints and talk philosophy. I was shocked when she asked me to teach her how to use hot hair rollers. Wouldn't a stage performer already know how to do that? Happily, she was a quick study, and I told her to help herself to my rollers, anytime.

My first real Stanford friend was Vicki Hahn down the hall. She was so blond and her eyes so blue, she sometimes caught me staring at her, like I'd never seen blue eyes before. (And except for Ellie, I rarely had!) She basically took me by the proverbial hand and immersed me in Stanford campus life. The Big Game, the Stanford Band, frat parties (when I was at Stanford, sororities were banned from campus because of a suicide years earlier), sunning at Lake Lagunita and catching rides with upperclassmen into the city (San Francisco). Not a word about Club Med, Piaget or Vail. Turns out, Vicki was the daughter of a wealthy rice farmer from Colusa County, CA. She grew up driving her dad's air-conditioned harvester through acres of rice. She skied, but stayed close to home — at Lake Tahoe, not Vail. She taught me how to drive her stick shift Mustang and never once called me out for grinding her gears. We laughed our heads off when we ate gooey pizza from the Oasis and washed it down with TAB diet cola. Boy, were we watching our calories or what?? The thing about Vicki was that she had ALWAYS wanted to go to Stanford, so she knew everything about it. MemChu (Memorial Church), the Dollies, even SLAC (the Stanford Linear Accelerator). I had fallen into the school, hoping its intellectual reputation would rub off on me. I was in for a shock. I got the first D in my life on a math quiz. It wasn't even a 100 Level course, more of a remedial math class. I also got Cs on my human biology and other quizzes. My humiliation was complete. I was indeed an admissions mistake.

I doubled down for finals. I decided to teach myself how to study for and take tests. I spent many Friday and Saturday nights in UGLY (Undergraduate Library) at a drafty carrel by the window. For my math final, I eked out a B-. My report card had no Ds. I breathed a sigh of relief. Thankfully, I did okay in classes that required writing. That's when I decided a Communication major combined with American Studies was probably where I should be headed. I started volunteering at the *Stanford Daily* office as a reporter. The student editors there taught me the trade, more so than anything I learned in my journalism classes. Ledes, present tense, pyramid style, "I said ten inches (of copy) not twelve!" they shouted. John C. Freed, Stephen L. Carter, Mark Funk, Bonny Rodden and Dan Fiduccia were scary-fun to work with. The *Stanford Daily* was serious business. It was a daily, so the editors demanded nothing but your best. They marked up each day's issue with red wax pencil pointing out misspellings, misleading headlines, poorly written ledes and story placement. Some late nights, after we put the paper to bed, we brought back Jack Steak sandwiches and greasy onion rings, the stale odors lingering in the newsroom for days.

I couldn't believe that so many of the professors and researchers on campus would agree to an interview when I told them I was a reporter at *The Daily.* Whatever the time, I jumped on my bike and pedaled to their office or home. More often, they'd just talk to me on the phone. "I can't believe they just talked to me," I said, hanging up the receiver. "This journalism thing just might work."

Despite the late nights, my grades weren't suffering. Instead of taking regular science classes to fulfill my distribution, I signed up for "Physics for Poets" and "An Introduction to Solar Power." My solar power instructor even commented, "Your paper on how solar panels work was good. You should think of becoming a reporter!" Check!

My mom and dad were slightly alarmed by my phone call my sophomore year.

"You're taking a class from who?" asked Dad. I told him I had a class taught by the Black activist and communist, Angela Davis.

"Is she becoming a hippie?" I could hear mom in the background shouting from the kitchen. For some reason, my mom had a huge fear of me becoming a "hippie" because I was going to school so close to San Francisco, which was Hippie Haven in her mind.

Turns out they had little to fear. Ms. Davis was teaching a class on the labor movement and oppression of minority groups. I actually went to see her during office hours, and she told me to my great surprise that being a journalist was not a profession, but rather a craft, a union job. She went on — you are part of the working class, easily exploitable by publishers, that's why you need the union. And, she added, you are a minority woman. Expect to face a double dose of discrimination.

I don't recall what grade I got for that class, but it opened my eyes to the larger world of race and class that awaited outside The Farm. There were ethnic theme houses on campus — Zapata with a LatinX focus, Ujamaa for those interested in African American themes and Junipero (renamed Okada House in 1979) with an Asian American focus. Being from Hawai'i, I had no desire to live in an Asian American themed house. I'd just come from a place crawling with Asian Americans! But I did find myself visiting the People's Tea House for *char siu bao* and hot tea once in a while. And during conversations there, I was surprised that many students had large gaps in their knowledge of their heritage and customs.

Growing up in Hawai'i, folks were surrounded by other people's customs. My experience was proof. I had a Japanese name and wore *yukata* during the summer, danced Hawaiian hula, loved eating Korean *kalbi* and *kimchi*, watched Chinese kung fu movies and ate candied lotus root during Lunar New Year and hung out at Carlton's house where we ate Filipino pancit and chicken adobo. Everyone I knew could speak a few words of the other person's ethnic language (usually a greeting so you could be polite to their immigrant grandparents or order food at a restaurant). What shocked me the most was hearing Japanese Americans pronouncing Japanese words and names with what I called a "mainland" accent. Some of the most egregious examples were "kerr rotty" (*karate*) and "carry oakie" (*karaoke*). Didn't their parents teach them the correct way to say these words? Some even mispronounced their Japanese surnames.

An epiphany would soon come. In 1973, Jeanne Wakatsuki Houston published her memoir, *Farewell to Manzanar*, which described her family's experience before, during and after their incarceration in Manzanar concentration camp during World War II. Back in high school, I may have heard passing mention of such "camps," but until Wakatsuki's book exploded on the scene, it was just that, a murmur, a whisper.

Hawai'i had never seen the mass incarceration of Japanese Americans like they did on the Mainland. There, 120,000 people of Japanese ancestry, most of them American citizens, were uprooted from their homes, schools and businesses by the U.S. government and imprisoned in desolate camps for no crime and without due process. We learned later that fewer than two thousand people from Hawai'i were also rounded up and sent to camps located on several of the islands or on the Mainland. My own grandfather, Masaji Matsukawa, on the island of Kaua'i was sent to Kalaheo camp from his home in Kekaha as a security threat. I was told he was the plantation scribe and communicated with the Japanese Consulate in Honolulu because he was one of the few who could read and write. That made him a security threat. He spent at least eight months away from his family but was let go for health reasons.

The sheer number of Japanese in Hawai'i helped insulate them from the racist and unconstitutional dragnet happening along the West Coast beginning in the spring of 1942. Nearly 159,000 persons of Japanese ancestry lived in Hawai'i at the time of the Pearl Harbor attack, more than thirty-five percent of the population. Officers in the U.S. Navy at Pearl Harbor and the Army's Commanding General in Hawai'i, Delos Emmons, urged restraint and argued against incarcerating more Hawai'i Japanese because they were necessary for the war effort. That's why my mom's father and brothers weren't drafted and still had plenty of gasoline for their trucks. They ran a dairy — vital to the war effort!

Which brings me back to the Mainland accents among so many of the Mainland Japanese Americans. After spending years in a concentration camp, Japanese Americans coming home to an often hostile and racist neighborhood told me it was simply uncool to be Japanese. Families abandoned Japanese customs and language. Looking, speaking and even eating like a Japanese person made you "the enemy." The idea was to "Be American" which meant being white and speaking English. The concentration camp experience — and how it psychologically wounded thousands of Japanese Americans — would loom large in my journalism career. I now understood and accepted the Mainland accent and was grateful my family had escaped that fate.

As the Stanford campus began to grapple with a

burgeoning ethnic awareness movement, I was approached in the *Daily* office by another reporter named Bill Sing. His big idea was to start an Asian American newspaper to cover topics like ethnic studies, housing discrimination in San Francisco and the general civil rights movement as it affected Asian Americans. I agreed to be a reporter and associate editor. When I told my mother about this new "project" she cried out, "Why are you working on this radical newspaper? Are you becoming a hippie?"

Again, I never understood what hippie-dom meant to her. But I sensed our old friend *haji* — fear of shame — in her voice. *What would people say about you working for such a newspaper?* I could only imagine that she thought editing a "radical" newspaper was NOT what a former Miss Teenage America would do and certainly not what a good Japanese daughter would do. I decided to work on the paper anyway. I just wouldn't send her any copies.

Bill and I worked on the publication right in the *Daily* office. The *Daily* staff pretty much left us alone as we labored on what was basically a community newspaper. And again, my experience growing up as part of the "majority" (Japanese) in Hawai'i was crashing into the experience of most Asian Americans in the Bay Area, who were definitely in the "minority." Many of the Asian Americans living in San Francisco were poor. Many of the elderly spoke no English and lived in shabby Chinatown apartments. Word got out that the residents of the "I-Hotel" (International Hotel) were going to be forcibly evicted to make way for redevelopment. Our community newspaper, which we called *Winds*, covered some of the skirmishes between activists trying to keep the mostly low-income Filipino tenants in their home and the City of San Francisco. I was witnessing a social movement involving students, Asian American leaders and labor unions growing more intense by the day. As crazy as it sounds, Bill and I got into a huge argument over whether to call the tenants Filipinos or Pilipinos.

"It's Filipinos, with an "f," I insisted. "That's what we say in Hawai'i."

"It's Pilipinos, with a "p," Bill shot back. "That's what they call themselves."

"But in America, we call their land the Philippines, with an "f" sound. So they are Filipinos!" I argued. Bill wouldn't budge.

"So do we call it a farking lot?" I demanded. "Do they play pootball? Because that's what they say!" I began to think this was a weird conversation.

In the end, we used Pilipinos. But I never did say it out loud.

On August 4, 1977, 400 police officers began to remove the tenants in the I-Hotel. They were confronted by three thousand protestors who had surrounded and barricaded the building. Within six hours, the remaining fifty-five tenants were evicted. Because it was summer, I wasn't there to witness the clash. My mother thought it was just as well.

CHAPTER 9
THE INTERN

Whenever college students ask me for advice about becoming a journalist, I ask them if they have had an internship. It's shocking to me *even today* that some of them haven't had one or don't even know what an internship is. I have to stop myself from grabbing them and shouting, "Then get one! And don't you dare graduate from college without one!"

I was fortunate to be selected for an internship at the *Honolulu Advertiser* the summer of my sophomore and junior years. All those hours at the *Stanford Daily* office were paying off. I had a folder of articles I had written. I knew how to set up and do phone interviews. And I could write on deadline. I was surrounded and encouraged by real, live reporters and editors. I even shared the same newsroom with veteran reporter Beverly Creamer, who had written the article about my return to Hawai'i as Miss Teenage America three years earlier!

My first assignment was to write obituaries from forms families had filled out. Not the most interesting job, but it made me curious about cremation. I pitched and eventually wrote a feature on the process and the ways people bid aloha to their loved one's remains. I learned the bones can be pulverized from granular to powder to accommodate different sized urns.

As a general assignment reporter, I experienced all kinds of events and people. I interviewed a *kahuna* (a friend of mine from the Aiea Swinging Singers) about ancient chanting styles, including the technique of chanting in one's throat. I flew in a glider — basically, a plane with NO ENGINE. I reviewed art exhibits, attended zoning commission meetings and described accident scenes.

But I also got a harsh lesson in conflict of interest and drawing boundaries for myself. Ultimately, it meant I couldn't have a journalism career in the Islands. No one told me about "conflict of interest" as it pertained to journalism. Perhaps the professional reporters I worked with knew about it but didn't think to tell the intern about it. I realize now I should have spoken up when I began to feel anxious about what I was being asked to do and the repercussions to come.

An investigative reporter on staff was doing a story on political patronage. Did I know anyone who got a summer job because of his or her "connections" to a certain city councilmember? I said yes and was asked to interview that person. I should have stopped it right there. Not only was this a clear conflict because I knew the person, but my father had campaigned for the city councilmember in question. When I brought my concerns to the reporter, he asked, "Is what you heard and wrote about true? Is it what was told to you?" I said yes, but what I should have added was "And I feel damned uncomfortable about it." No surprise that when the article came out, my parents were furious. It made their council friend look bad. *Haji* (shame)!

"You shouldn't have participated in that story," scolded my mother. She was right about that!

"You have shamed our family." It was like a dagger to my heart.

Mom had spent her life warning me about *haji* and how it must be avoided at all costs. Saving face and keeping up appearances was paramount in Japanese culture. It's why Japanese don't talk about alcoholism, domestic violence, unplanned pregnancies, bankruptcy or jail time even within their own families.

Now, I could have argued that many residents were probably glad to read this story. Their children may not have gotten summer jobs because they weren't well connected. But enlightenment for the masses brought shame and dishonor to our family. My parents lost face with the councilmember because of me. From that moment, I knew my work as a journalist would have to flourish elsewhere. Working in Hawai'i would always be bound in a web of *on*, obligation.

I was quite happy preparing for my life as a print journalist. But things were about to change. My managing editor, Mike Middlesworth, strolled to my desk one day and said, "Have you ever thought about doing TV news?" He looked at me and lowered his voice. "You know, they're hiring women these days."

I looked up at him, a bit surprised.

"I never thought about it," I replied.

"Well, think about it," he said as he continued his newsroom patrol. "You have a nice voice."

As soon as I got back to Stanford my senior year, I started combing the Comm Department for information on television internships. There was one at KPIX in San Francisco, a short train ride up the Peninsula. I snagged it and for two nights a week in Fall Quarter, I wrote scripts and answered phones in the KPIX newsroom. It was a more brutal office than the laidback *Honolulu Advertiser.* The show producer I worked for, Rose Krupp, chain smoked thin, brown cigarettes that clung to her well-glossed lips. I was so afraid she would drop ashes on the scripts and start a fire.

She tore some AP wire copy off the teletype and

demanded, "Take this and write me 20 seconds!" My confused expression made her pause.

"You know how to write copy, right?" she sighed.

"Helpful tips?" I asked, as I had never written a broadcast script before.

She rolled her eyes. "Present tense. Active speech. Short sentences. And don't go long!" That was pretty much the only instruction I ever got for television news writing.

After laboring for thirty minutes on a twenty second story, I brought her my script. She grabbed it. Read it, her thin, brown cigarette quivering. Then, RRRIPPP! She tore it in half and tossed it in the trash.

"Too long! And use simple words!" she snapped and went back to her rundown.

I came back a second time. Rrrip! Again, not good enough.

Finally, she kept the third script. Didn't even grunt out a thank you.

I watched the newscast and smiled when my story appeared. But that smile vanished when, after the newscast, the anchor woman stormed into the newsroom.

"Who wrote this?" she demanded. She looked at me and at the show producer.

"You don't level a gun," she angrily shook the copy. "You POINT a gun!" She stomped off in a flourish.

The producer looked at me and said in a snarky way. "Yeah, and she should have read her script ahead of time!" I nodded, "Yeah." We got along a lot better after that.

Some of the reporters were *prima donnas*, too. One afternoon as I was answering phones, a male reporter called and yelled, "Let me speak to Rose!"

"Rose isn't at her desk," I said. "Can I take a message?"

The reporter paused, then began shouting. "Wha... who is this? Let me speak to someone who knows something! I don't want to speak to a CETA worker!" (CETA stood for the Comprehensive Employment and Training Act, a job training program for poor people.) I was shaken but turned his call over to another desk assistant. What the hell? I swore I'd never be mean to anyone on the news desk, ever! Even to interns.

One reporter, however, took me under her wing. Wendy Tokuda came to KPIX TV from KING TV in Seattle, her hometown. She was one of those remarkable talents who started as an administrative assistant and worked her way up to a reporting position. She then jumped ten market sizes to San Francisco. When I asked if I could shadow her one day, she was quick to say yes and off we went. Wendy later told me she job shadowed Barbara Tanabe over at KOMO, the first Japanese American television reporter in the Seattle market.

"When she came on TV my dad would yell, 'BARBARA IS ON!!!'" and we'd all run to the front room to watch," recalled Wendy. "Anyway, she let me shadow her one morning and that's how I knew I wanted to be a reporter. So I owe a debt, right? People really lifted me, and now it's my turn to lift you."

Decades later, as I was preparing to retire, I took a young Cambodian American woman on a tour of Seattle's Chinatown-International District. She confessed shyly that I was quite the celebrity at her house.

"Everytime you came on TV, my dad called out, "LORI'S ON!," she giggled. "We loved watching another Asian on the news!" The tour became so much more meaningful for me. Being there made a difference!

Wendy was down to earth and her co-workers liked her, which was a very good thing for me. She introduced me to her photographer and her editor. This was crucial, as I needed to put together an audition tape before I left the internship if I ever wanted to get a job. Stanford had NO broadcast program, and therefore, no television equipment. Thanks to file video I dug up in the KPIX archives, the kindness of Wendy, photographer Lorne Morrison and editor Les Keeney,

I left KPIX with a videotape with a SINGLE story about earthquake safety. Les showed me how to make copies of the story on cassettes I purchased down the street.

It was the end of Winter Quarter, and I realized I had enough credits to graduate early. I couldn't wait to start working. I thirsted for a real job, reporting real stories and earning some real money. Although, as any journalist knows, your first job doesn't pay squat because you're starting out in a small market.

I mailed out a hundred resumes to both print and television markets across the western U.S. I was very conservative about sending any of my precious video cassettes since some television directors never returned them. I attached to each resume a small black and white photo taken by a friend of mine in the *Daily* newsroom. I thought if they liked what they saw, they would ask for the video. I thought the photo looked quite smart. I had my glasses perched atop my head and I sat near a typewriter. Who wouldn't hire me? Turns out, nearly everyone.

I only got two positive responses. One was for an entry level business reporting position at the *Los Angeles Times*. The other, for a reporting position at a tiny television station in Redding, California. I had to look for the town on a map and called the Greyhound station to ask if they even went there.

The LA Times position didn't require an in-person interview. The television position at KRCR required a screen test — in person. So I took the Greyhound to Redding and met the news director, Ian Evans. He was a friendly, round man who wore a gold watch and no necktie unless he was on air. He was also the station's weatherman. He asked me to write three stories from wire copy and move down to the studio to read them from the news set. There was no teleprompter, so I just had to keep looking down at my scripts to read the stories. There was no time to memorize anything.

"That's fine," said Ian after the taping was done. And

then, he shared the sobering details of the job. If hired, I would be the only reporter for the station based in Redding. Mike was the reporter based in nearby Chico. The 5 o'clock anchors, Clarissa Howland and Rand Oertle, would do some reporting, as would Ian. Clarissa produced the show, and Dave Andrade would cruise in at mid-day to put together the sports report. I would be the only person in the newsroom to produce and anchor the 11 o'clock newscast and cover any breaking news. Everyone had to shoot and edit their own SILENT 16mm film. The audio track was recorded on an 8-track sized cassette that was simul-rolled with the silent film live from the control room. The news story was basically assembled LIVE on the air as viewers watched. There were daily arguments over who would get to use the only video camera — a small Panasonic attached to a recorder the size of a mini fridge. The station was so "cost conscious" it didn't spring for compact batteries that fit into the recorder. Instead, the engineers rigged up a car battery into a case to lug along with the recorder. All the gear had to be loaded into a stick-shift Chevy Chevette with no air conditioning. Keep in mind, it gets very hot in Redding in the summer. That summer, the heat melted the cassette cover of the recorder, which was sitting in the hatchback. Oh, and the salary was ten thousand dollars.

I had a big decision to make. Here I was, pacing around the Greyhound station in Redding thinking: LA Times? Redding? LA Times? Redding? I picked Redding and here was my reasoning. Television reporting obviously needed a young person with strong arms to carry camera gear around. I would do television reporting first. Then, when I was toothless and wrinkled, I would be a print reporter because readers couldn't see what I looked like. It made perfect sense!

I packed a suitcase and my dormitory bedding into a used, bright orange Chevy Monza "Uncle" Manny helped negotiate and drove north to Redding in spring of 1978.

CHAPTER 10
TV NEWS — CRASH COURSE

My first day of work at KRCR in two words: crash course.

"Do you know how to shoot film?" news director Ian Evans asked. I shook my head. "No."

"Okay, here's your camera. It's a Bolex. You just crank it here to make it go." Ian turned the crank.

"Open it here and load your film. In here, through here, press the trigger." He loaded the film.

"I don't have a light meter for you. But if you're shooting outdoors, put your aperture on f16." He turned the aperture to f16. "If it's indoors, make it f8. And if the lighting indoors is fluorescent, slip this in the slot." He dug an orange filter out of his desk.

"Then hold it up, look through the viewfinder and shoot!" He squinted into the viewfinder.

"You can probably get three stories out of each hundred-foot roll of film," he mused.

"What if I want audio in the story?" I asked.

"Oh, you get THAT on your cassette recorder. You play it back when you are tracking your narration for the story."

What that meant was any background sound — like fire

truck sirens, twittering birds or babbling brooks — had to be recorded separately on a cassette. Then back in the sound booth, I had to blend the recorded sound with my voice onto an audio cartridge. It also meant interviews would never be filmed, just recorded on my audio cassette recorder. So I had to keep my interviews very short, as I only had a hundred feet of film to cover whatever was said.

"If you have to interview someone, just get the video camera," suggested Ian. "Carissa knows we all have to share."

Thank goodness I didn't have to develop the film. There was an engineer at the station who did that for everyone. But it meant everyone had to have their film in by early afternoon so he could develop it. Then, Carissa, Rand, Dave and I wrassled over who would edit their film first at the one editing bench. I got another crash course on film editing, learning new words such as viewer, emulsion, cutter and frames per second. And if, by chance, I was lucky enough to get the video camera, I learned videotape editing, too. Laying my audio track and background sound was relatively easy, as I had done reel-to-reel recording and editing at the Stanford University radio station, KZSU. Compared to that, the cassettes we recorded at KRCR were a cinch. One button to record, same one to stop. If you made a mistake, you pulled the cassette, degaussed it and started all over again.

After paying for rent and a cleaning deposit, I had very little money. My first week of work, I lived off a loaf of bread and a jar of peanut butter. I drank coffee with sugar and cream at the office because it was free. That first paycheck was magical. I went to Safeway and relished buying a pound of hamburger and a box of spaghetti.

I worked hard at KRCR. I suspect most journalists in their first jobs do. For many of us at the station, this was our first TV job, and we wanted to do well and learn. There were infuriating days when my film came out of the processor totally blue because I forgot to put in the orange filter at the council meeting. There were panicky days when I barely made my time slot because my interview subject gave me bad driving directions to their home. ("Go a couple miles and turn left where the old oak tree used to be." Seriously, who does this?) There were the hilarious nights when we opened the barn doors to the studio because it was so hot and large mosquito-eaters would slowly fly in and land on me during a newscast. Car crashes, wildfires, historical pieces and "celebrity" interviews (okay, it was with singer Anne Murray, but I thought she was a big deal!) were all part of the experience. I learned how to videotape myself to include in my stories. This was important because I was already putting together my new "audition reel." All the "newbies" at the station hung out together on our days off. And because we were all living on minimum wage, we did things that were free or low cost like hiking in the beautiful Shasta County countryside, playing tennis, rafting on Shasta Lake and having dance parties at each other's apartments.

There were just two of us newbies on the late-night shift responsible for the newscast at 11. Larry Blackstock was my director during the evening newscasts and ran the rest of the station before and after them. Each weeknight, I produced a late news rundown, deciding which stories to include and in what order. I had to time the segments so we could run all the commercial breaks and get on and off the air on time. Larry was in the control room while I was on the news set. He called out camera shots over a loudspeaker during the commercial breaks as we didn't have a way to communicate through earpieces. He also rolled the film chain, audio carts, videotape cassettes and reel to reel commercials, opened and closed my microphone and told me whether to look at Camera One or Camera Two. There was no teleprompter so I prayed my paper scripts wouldn't blow away on the few nights the air conditioner froze so we had to open the studio barn doors to cool the set.

Originally from Seattle, Larry was hired just a few months before me. In fact, he recorded my audition during my first visit to the station. He remembered how I stumbled over a word and thought, "Oh they're not going to hire that girl." Today, he says, "I'm glad they did."

At the time, we didn't know where the relationship would go. We enjoyed learning about each other. He juggled and did magic tricks. We played tennis and a board game called "Mastermind." It was a relationship built on trust. I trusted him to make the newscast that I was producing and anchoring happen. He trusted me to follow his directions and "turn on a dime" if a change had to be made.

Less than a year in, I was putting together a new audition tape for my next move. It was a surprise to no one. It's not that I didn't enjoy Redding, but most small market stations know they are stepping stones for folks seeking to work in larger markets. Larry and I talked about where to send my tape, and I decided I'd apply to stations up and down the West Coast like San Diego or Seattle rather than east to Las Vegas or Phoenix. I was able to put some anchoring on the tape and my prized story that I sold to ABC network about firefighting "smokejumpers" who trained near Redding. I must have broken a thousand OSHA regulations climbing the tower to get shots of the trainees jumping down the zipline. I needed to get that close because I was using my SILENT film camera that did not have a zoom lens.

In 1979, I accepted a job at KPTV, an independent station in Portland, Oregon. I was so happy to have jumped fifty or so market sizes to a "big city." The news director was a jovial man with spectacles, a bow tie and a firm handshake.

"Billll Swwiiiiinnng!" he introduced himself in his musical way.

Working at KPTV was at once delightful and dismaying.

We had photographers to shoot and edit the 16mm SOUND film. But we had no videotape cameras or a microwave truck for live shots. There were at least five veteran reporters but they all worked the day shift. So I was still stuck covering nightside council meetings, rushing back to get the film into the "soup" and finish co-producing the 10 p.m. newscast. There was no computer technology, so we had to backtime the news stories in our heads and type our scripts on multiply carbon paper. Still no teleprompter, so each evening, I watched enviously as the competition flashed their live shots from their microwave trucks and obviously read from teleprompters. It didn't help that our director had a drinking problem and some nights it really showed.

Up until now, I had never experienced in-your-face racism. I happened to answer the phone in the newsroom on the night of December 7th.

"KPTV Newsroom. Lori speaking."

The voice on the other end croaked, "Lori. Lori who?"

Not thinking anything was amiss, I said, "Lori Matsukawa."

"Matsu...is that a Jap name?" the caller asked angrily.

A bit shaken, I responded, "What do you want?"

"I want to shoot JAPS!" the male caller went on. I thought he sounded like a senior citizen.

"You Japs bombed Pearl Harbor. Started the damn war!" He was getting louder. "Why, if I had my gun I'd walk down the street with my rifle and shoot all the Japs I see!"

My shock must have been showing because the African American writer next to me looked up and whispered, "What is it??"

By now, the man was ranting about shooting Japs and coming to the station. I think the writer must have overheard him.

"Just hang up! Hang up!" she hissed. I hung up.

"Boy, I've never been yelled at like *that* before," I said, wringing my shaking hands.

"Those kind, they're just ignorant. Just hang up on them," she huffed. "You okay?"

I nodded but still felt queasy inside. What would cause someone to do that? I was an American, not a Jap. And that's when it dawned on me — the Japanese Americans along the entire West Coast (including Oregon) were put in wartime American concentration camps because they were mistaken for Japanese nationals — the enemy! It made me angry. That caller didn't believe I was an American! There was no mistaking the message. "You don't belong here. I want to kill you." Thank goodness for my understanding colleague. I wish I could remember her name. The stories she could have told me about being judged by the color of one's skin.

Soon after that frightening incident, Larry got a job at KGW across town. It was the first time a guy had purposely followed me to a television market to stay close. I liked that. We were able to hang out and on weekends, drive up to Seattle to explore his favorite haunts like Pike Place Market and Seattle Center, home of the Space Needle. Portland is a lovely city but it has a chilly downside — freezing rain. That particular winter, there was a doozy of a storm that swept through the Dalles and covered Portland in an inch of ice. Tree branches, bridges, roads, everything was coated with ice. A woman died when an ice-coated tree branch fell on her. It took me an hour to chip the ice around my car door with a screwdriver and hammer so I could get in and start the heater to melt the rest of the ice. I was done with this weather!

It turns out, nature wasn't done with me. I felt queasy several mornings in a row, so I took a pregnancy test. The stick showed "Positive." I gasped and slumped on the toilet seat.

"Oh no! This can't be happening!" My mind raced back to

a night where Larry and I had an epic prophylactic fail. "What are we going to do?"

My world was crashing around me. I began to panic.

"I'm only twenty-three. There's no way I'm ready to raise a child! My career! This is just my second television market on my way to the big time. I can't make it there as a single mother with a child. Single! I loved Larry, but we hadn't really talked about getting married. Was I going to be the pregnant bride, waddling down the aisle, being judged by friends and relatives?"

Two decades of *haji* indoctrination echoed through my mind.

"Don't bring shame to your family. What a slut, having sex before marriage and worse, getting pregnant as a result! How dare you waste that education your parents paid for! You know they had to take a second mortgage out on the house. You … have …failed. "

I picked up the phone and called a clinic.

"Are abortions legal in Oregon?" I asked the woman who answered the phone.

"Yes, they are," she said. I thanked her and hung up.

Larry and I had a talk when he got home from work. I was frightened and sad. He was worried and said whatever I decided, he would support me. This was the lowest I'd ever been in my life, but I felt I still had a choice.

I refused to bring a child into the world who was not one hundred percent wanted and one hundred percent supported. I wanted to give that child every advantage, including a mother and father who were married and raising that child together under the same roof. I would not settle for just "any old job" because I knew I could be a broadcast journalist in a larger market — possibly at the network — and I refused to give up on that dream. And thanks to *Roe v. Wade* and women's health advocates, abortions were legal in Oregon. I can only write this now that both my parents have passed. It would bring them such shame that their daughter could disrespect them in this way. But this is America, not Japan. I was willing to live with the consequences of my choice. Years later, Larry and I were married and blessed with a healthy baby boy. I thanked God for the chance to be the wife and mother I knew I could be. I only know that when faced with disaster, disappointment or few good choices, I listen to that voice in me. Experiencing a setback did not make me a failure. It made me human. I forced myself to get up in front of the world, and declare, "Look. This is who I am. Not perfect, but who is?"

CHAPTER 11
MOM AND THE VOLCANO

Months later, I heard from the assistant news director at KOMO TV in Seattle of an opening for a reporter. I jumped at it. I told Howard Scott that I wasn't usually this flighty but I really needed to get out of Portland. He said come on up. I left KPTV after working there for just ten months.

When I drove up to KOMO my first day of work, I looked up and saw the Space Needle, glistening above me. I felt like Mary in the show-open of the "Mary Tyler Moore Show" where she twirls around and tosses her hat in the air. I was at a big market TV station! As I walked through the newsroom, I beamed at all the big market toys I encountered. Computers at all the producer desks. A newsroom camera for live shots. A row of photographers editing their film or videotape stories at the edit bench. (KOMO was just transitioning to all-videotape production). A teleprompter! Other staff whose only job was to write, to edit tape, to monitor the radio scanners or collect audio for the photographer — all of them doing some of the work I had to do myself.

Being the newbie meant working weekends. But it paid off in spades one Sunday morning, May 18, 1980.

Mount Saint Helens erupted.

Our crew was taking an early morning flight in a small, fixed wing to the Washington coast to do a feature on clam digging. The pilot suddenly called back, "We have to turn around! The mountain blew up!"

Photographer Kevin Kelly, audio technician Maybin Baker and I looked out our windows and gasped.

"Holy crap!" yelled Maybin.

Mount Saint Helens was spewing a huge plume of gray ash! The plume climbed higher and higher into the sky, a furious, boiling, ever widening expanse of gray that covered the sky. I looked down and saw a river turned gray. My heart began pounding. So much power in that roiling ash cloud. I gasped as I saw a pickup truck and tree trunks swept downstream. "People must have died," I thought.

"My God," was all I could utter.

The pilot put down at Chehalis-Centralia Airport. We got our marching orders from the newsroom. Stay there! We're sending news cars and microwave trucks!

The next week was a blur. KOMO kept several of us reporters in Chehalis, using it as a base camp for Mount Saint Helens coverage. It was hard to get information. How many died? How many are still missing? Which roads are closed?

I was eager to cover the aftermath, but also fearful that the ash around us would be bad for our lungs and the news car air filters. We had never experienced an ash eruption like this before.

We interviewed residents who lived miles away, their yards and rooftops covered with ash. We talked to motorists who couldn't travel along Interstate-5 because volcanic mud and debris destroyed the roadway or slammed into bridges, possibly compromising them. When I got back to the station a week later, I finally saw the amazing film footage shot by our colleague, Dave Crockett, Jr. He was actually swept up in the mud and ash in the eruption! He had gone to the mountain that morning because everyone had been reporting for days how the eruption was "imminent." The footage was dark because the ash turned day into night. With the news car's alarm crying in the background, we saw what Dave saw as he hiked away in waist-deep mud, his camera rolling. He kept talking, cussing and said he hoped someone would find this film and develop it because he didn't think he would make it out alive. He eventually did get to higher ground and was rescued. Others were not so lucky. Fifty-seven people died in the blast which, according to the U.S. Geological Survey, was the deadliest and most economically destructive volcanic event in U.S history.

Not every reporting day would be as dramatic as Mount St. Helens, although I nearly lost a photographer, audio technician and video camera doing a feature on a proposed horseback riding trail in the Auburn area. For some reason, I thought we needed a "point of view" shot between the horse's ears as it plodded along the trail. Photographer Steve Duex and audio tech John Rieber each got on a horse and headed down the trail with Steve's camera cable connected to the recorder in John's lap. Why we thought this was a good idea is beyond me. Suddenly, Steve's horse got spooked and galloped away, with Steve clutching his camera for dear life. I remember seeing his hair flying back and his eyes wide open. The video cable tightened and snapped out of the camera. It's amazing that John was able to stay on his horse as the recorder lurched him forward, then back. I was at once terrified and hysterical with laughter. It looked like something straight out of a movie! When we got back to the station, Steve said the managers were understanding, impressed even, with our initiative. However, we decided not to do fancy shots with animals ever again.

One of the drawbacks at KOMO was we didn't have a morning news show. Our crosstown competitor, KING, had a half hour at 6:30 a.m. So, we decided to start our own morning show. KOMO hired producer Susan Stearns and writer Lisa Yeakel and threw me and our weekend sports anchor Tony Ventrella up in front of the cameras. We called our show, "Wake Up." It was fun creating our news open featuring a showerhead, toaster and alarm clock that looked suspiciously like Susan's stuff. "Wake Up" didn't have a dedicated news crew. As far as the managers were concerned, reporter shifts started at 9 a.m. and ended at 11:30 p.m. Since we went on the air at 6:30 a.m. it was hard to get anyone to do live shots for us. Today, all the stations in town have morning news programs, most of which start at 4:30 a.m. And they have live shots!

With all the busy-ness involving work, my personal life was also demanding attention. While it seemed my co-workers were solely focused on their work, I was juggling family and romantic drama daily!

By 1981, Larry had moved up from Portland and began working at KOMO, too. We decided after hopscotching through three cities, it was time to get married. He surprised me with dinner and a ring with a view of the Monorail and the twinkling city lights. It was very Seattle. Of course, Susan and Lisa at work were ecstatic when I showed them the ring the next day, almost more excited than I was. I was nervous about getting married to a white Mainland guy who had recently stood up to Mom and Dad, but mostly Mom.

Months earlier, Larry and I became the targets of a mother's remorse.

My very improbable life path had made my parents, particularly my mother, very proud and at the same time fearful. Mom was the quintessential *Nisei* daughter. The youngest of eight siblings growing up in an immigrant household, Mom straddled the cultures of Meiji Era Japan and a burgeoning, brand new state called Hawai'i.

Would Flo be the obedient Japanese wife practicing superstitious customs from the old country? Mom still tossed salt over her shoulder before entering the house after attending a funeral (kept the evil spirits away). She scolded me when I left a knife on the stove (your children will have cleft palates). She told me never to sweep dust out of the house at night (sweeping away your fortune). And never kill a moth (it's the spirit of a deceased loved one visiting you). Her family didn't expect much from her — the "baby" of the family, especially a female one.

Or would Flo be the independent American woman who would cut her own path? Mom was the only one of her siblings to graduate from college and the only daughter to work outside the home as a school teacher. As she chaperoned me during my Miss Teenage America year, Mom was no doubt already envisioning the glorious possibilities for her *Sansei* (third generation) daughters. I could almost hear the thoughts going through her head:

"Lori's well-spoken, poised. She'll attend a prestigious college with her scholarship, marry a Japanese American doctor or perhaps an engineer. If she becomes a journalist, she will surely want to be a network star."

Mom's thinking about husbands for her daughters was tempered by the racist history of Hawai'i's plantation economy. Marrying Japanese would be the best scenario because they are YOUR people, a known quantity. Chinese would not be suitable unless their families were wealthy. Other Asian groups who came to the plantations after the Japanese (Koreans, Filipinos and Portuguese — who, of course, weren't Asian but worked on the plantations) were not desirable. African Americans? Definitely not. Their skin color was too dark, and their ancestors worked on plantations as well. And in a strange sort of compassion, she believed any children from such a marriage would suffer "extreme prejudice" from society. Too sad. Caucasians, so called *haoles*, might be considered because they held the *luna* or boss positions on the plantations and those above them basically ruled the Islands often by cheating or ingratiating themselves to the monarchy. The *kama'aina haoles* were the wealthy landowners, bankers and financiers who could elevate one's social status. So in essence, wealthy *haoles* passed the marriage test.

Mixed with those long-standing prejudices was the American definition of "success" as defined in the sexist Sixties and Seventies. In Mom's experience, women didn't need to work if their husbands made enough money. So, a woman had to marry a doctor or engineer who earned enough money so she could stay at home and not work. That also implied that the husband/doctor had a good education which would match, even exceed, his wife's. In Mom and Dad's case, the fact they were both University of Hawai'i-educated made up for the fact that they earned very little as public school teachers. Japanese society valued education. So, marrying a poor guy with a bachelor's degree trumped marrying the poor guy with no degree. And if marriage was not an immediate option, hey, it was the Seventies! Echoing my old managing editor at the *Advertiser*, Mom said, "They're hiring women now." A booming career would take the sting out of having a daughter who didn't get married until she was in her forties.

I believe Mom saw Larry and my strengthening relationship as a threat. He was, in her mind, taking me away from her. With each visit home, she sat me down at the kitchen table out of his hearing and said how sorry she was that she gave me so much independence.

"I really regret letting you leave here," she said. "Once you graduated from high school and went to the mainland, you were gone!"

"I'm not gone," I said brightly. "I still come home … a lot! I'll always come home."

"But I feel I don't have enough time to talk to you, to do things with you, I regret that I let you go," she mourned.

Sometimes, she called Dad over to join her.

He cleared his throat and said, "Lori, you should think

about your career. If you want to work your way up, you have to be independent so you can pick up and go."

Mom even played the education card. "You know, you went to Stanford and Larry only has an AA degree. Why didn't you choose one of the guys you dated at Stanford?" (This was before Larry went on to earn his BS in business and MA in pastoral studies while working full time.) This was her not-so-subtle way of saying, "Why couldn't you marry a doctor?"

It never seemed to occur to her that marrying a doctor had its own risks. In such a marriage, whose career would take precedence? Wouldn't we have to "settle down" in one place, which would bring my budding journalism career to a halt? I felt I was fortunate to have a fiancé in the same industry who had few qualms about moving to different television markets.

This went on for several trips home until the spring of 1981. I went ahead of Larry to spend a few days with the family before he joined me later. For three straight nights, I got the kitchen table talk. For three straight nights, I called Larry in tears, telling him we should probably break up. He should forget about coming to the Islands that weekend. I was so stressed out.

One morning, my youngest sister Liane, who was about fifteen at the time, answered a knock at the door.

There was Larry, with a suitcase at his side, the cab driving away. He had just taken a red-eye from Seattle to Hawai'i.

"Hi. Is Lori here?" he asked.

Liane's eyes got as big as saucers. "Uh … Lori!!" Liane turned and shouted. "Larry's here!"

Larry heard alarmed voices within the house. "Who? Larry?"

I ran to the door, curious about the commotion. Mom hurried from the other direction. We all three stood there, looking at Larry like he was a Martian.

"Hi!" I said, with a sigh of relief. "Come in!"

The next few days were difficult. There were many kitchen table talks with Larry and me with both parents, Larry and me with either parent, even Larry solo with first Dad then Mom. We took off for Kaua'i as planned for a few days. The relatives were sympathetic and assured us things would work out. "It's tough to be the first in the family to get married," mused one cousin.

Well, that's just the beginning, I thought. Larry was a Mainland *haole* who was still trying to finish his bachelor's degree in business and work at the same time. And his spur-of-the-moment flight to Hawai'i on a red-eye to support his girlfriend, well that was just impetuous! And yet …

As we took a long walk around the neighborhood, Larry kept saying gently, "Lori, I'm not trying to force you to stay with me. It's your decision. Just don't let your parents decide for you. I like what we have but what do YOU want? That's what matters."

I returned to Seattle with a heavy heart. I loved what Larry and I had. He was kind and loving. I saw the way he treated his mother with love and respect. He treated me that way! We were in the same industry and could make our job situations work, I knew that. And despite the rejection he endured at my parents' home in Hawai'i, he never spoke ill of them. Yet, I didn't want to defy my parents. In Japanese tradition, to disobey them would be shameful, especially for an eldest child who sets the example for the younger ones.

So there I stood, Susan and Lisa clapping excitedly and telling the entire newsroom staff the news: "Lori and Larry are engaged!" It was almost like the Miss Teenage America announcement, all over again. An announcement, all kinds of hubbub around me while I stand there in a bubble of silence, watching and wondering: what lies ahead?

There was some tension when I told my parents about the engagement. I just flat out told Mom and Dad we would be holding the wedding in Seattle at Blaine Memorial United Methodist Church, which had become Larry's and my church family. I, of course, wanted them to come since Lisa and Liane were going to be my bridesmaids and my cousin Kendra my matron of honor. I didn't hear back from my parents for several months. Lisa told me to just hang in there, "They'll come."

In the meantime, Larry and I pooled our savings for a gown and a lace hat/veil from Henrietta's Hats. I sewed my bridesmaids' dresses using yards of lavender voile. Larry's mom, Alice Blackstock, helped with the elastic and hemming. (Through our entire courtship, Alice never questioned Larry about marrying a Japanese American woman. When I asked her about it years later, she simply said, "Well, it was obvious you loved each other!") We called the University of Washington and located a student string quartet to play at the reception. We couldn't afford a sit-down dinner so we planned a small wine and hors d'oeuvres reception at The Spinnaker down at Shilshole Bay Marina. We hired a photographer who was just starting out, a friend of a friend sort of thing. We're lucky we even got a few group photos of the event. He was so green!

With the wedding just months away, Liane finally called and said, "Mom and Dad are coming." I was elated! We wrote Dad into the ceremony to walk me down the aisle. As we waited for the guests to arrive at the church, Mom took Larry aside and held his hand. "Welcome to the family," she said. Larry said his heart almost burst with happiness.

Until the day she died, Mom and Larry were buddies and co-conspirators in Matsukawa family life.

For all of Mom's plans and dreams, it turned out none of her daughters married a Japanese American. Lisa married a Chinese American from Seattle; Liane married a Caucasian from Kailua. And none of the three husbands ... was a doctor.

CHAPTER 12
BREAKING THE
COLOR BARRIER

After an overly ambitious honeymoon to Mexico City, Orlando and Guadeloupe French West Indies, it was time to refocus on work. I was assigned to cover the state legislature when it convened in January 1983. So, six months after our wedding, I was living in an Olympia motel five days a week filing reports for KOMO television and radio.

I had never done legislative reporting before and eagerly soaked up the wisdom of my legislative photographers, Bob Turner and Dave Mann. Bob took me on a tour of the Capitol, pointing out the printing office where all the bills came from, the governor's office, the basement cafeteria, "Ulcer Gulch" where all the lobbyists hung out and all the best galleries from which to shoot a live shot. I met the other legislative reporters and paid special attention to the radio folks. They had the ability to explain a complicated law in forty seconds including a short sound bite while I took a minute thirty seconds. It was a master's class in legislative reporting.

At first, I was leery of rubbing elbows with lobbyists because I knew they were paid to push their agenda. Yet, I learned they were also part of the law-making process and a valuable source of information. Robert S. Lasnik and William L. Downing were prosecutors for King County who taught me a lot about how they advocated for changes in the law. They were always willing to present me with several sides of an argument, which helped me write better news stories. I think working with a journalist also helped them explain things without using jargon or legalese. Bill became a King County Superior Court judge, the first jurist in the country to knock down the "Defense of Marriage Act" banning same gender marriage in 2004. Bob wrote a letter of recommendation for my application to graduate school at the University of Washington and was later appointed to the federal district court by President Clinton in 1998. I also met others who would rise to national prominence, although we didn't know it then. Ron Sims was a legislative aide to Senator George Fleming who helped create the Office of Minority and Women's Business Enterprises in 1983. Both Fleming and Sims were two of the few Blacks working in Olympia at the time. He knew "folks I should get to know" in the African American community whom I eagerly added to my Rolodex for future stories. In the following years, I found myself covering Sims as he became a member of the King County Council, then King County Executive and later, deputy secretary of the US Department of Housing and Urban Development under President Barack Obama.

Gary Locke was a member of the House and headed the Budget Committee. He was one of just a couple of Asian Americans in the legislature at the time (the other was Art Wang, a representative from Tacoma). I liked interviewing Locke because he was able to explain complex issues in plain English. Little did I know that he would eventually become governor and later serve as U.S. commerce secretary and ambassador to China under President Obama.

I learned that Locke was a mentee of Ruth Yoneyama Woo. Meeting her, one would never know the cheery, smiling woman behind the big glasses was the "Godmother of Asian American politics" — one of the most influential behind-the-scenes actors in state campaigns. Many would-be politicians first sat with Ruth at her kitchen table to get her blessing and advice. She was adamant that as elected officials, they support communities of color. Among her protegees were Democrats Gary Locke, Ron Sims, Sharon Tomiko Santos, Bob Hasegawa and Ed Murray. Among her admirers were her former boss, U.S. Senator Dan Evans, and former Secretary of State Ralph Munro, both Republicans. What was growing before my eyes was a generation of public servants and activists who were claiming a place at the table for communities of color. I was enthralled. I wanted to get to know these communities and their leaders. Little did I know then that the issues of race and equity they were rallying around would personally affect me very soon.

While I got a great journalism education working at KOMO, I saw my path to promotion as a news anchor blocked by what I could only surmise as racial discrimination and preservation of the status quo. At the time (about 1983) KOMO was in a battle for ratings with cross-town rival, KING. So when KOMO's main five o'clock anchor Ruth Walsh left the news desk, managers replaced her with Kathy Goertzen, who was the same age as me. Kathy had blond hair and blue eyes and greatly resembled KING's longtime five o'clock anchor, Jean Enersen — just younger. Jean told me later that for decades after that, people on the street often confused the two of them, calling out Kathy's name instead of hers. Kathy told me the same thing. People called her Jean. In the ensuing decades, Kathy, Jean and I accepted that our roles as women news anchors in Seattle would be awkward at times. We would be civil about things and be role models for other women aspiring to become broadcast journalists. That was important because in the early 1980s, the visibility and promotion of women in television news was in its infancy. Sadly, Kathy died of an incurable brain tumor in 2012.

KOMO managers selected another Caucasian woman for the weekend and fill-in duties, a brunette named Kerry Brock. Meanwhile, Connie Thompson (who is Black) and I were pretty much left out of the anchorwoman sweepstakes even though we both had done anchoring duties there before. What made this even more frustrating was that the decisions were being made by our news director — who was a white woman! When I asked her about opportunities for advancement, she was noncommittal, saying they "might come up eventually." I decided I didn't want to wait around. Turns out, a former KOMO reporter we staffers affectionately called "McGruff" would be my ticket out.

It was the summer of 1983. Crime reporter John Sandifer had a gruff, authoritative voice as well as a hangdog expression. An unlit cigarette hung from his lips, and he always wore a trench coat. He resembled McGruff the Crime Dog, a registered trademark of the National Crime Prevention Council. So he called himself McGruff the News Hound. He was passionate about tracking down dirty cops, serial killers and racketeers. He was also a union shop steward and (shades of Angela Davis) explained to me the importance of union protection in the highly subjective and competitive news business.

He called one day after jumping ship from KOMO to KING. Would I be interested in having lunch with the new news director at KING? Sandifer was the producer of the station's new concept show. I was game to meet the legendary Don Dunkel, the former ABC field producer who personally set up the satellite connections each night in Tehran for Ted Koppel's coverage of the Iran hostage crisis. (In November 1979, fifty-two American diplomats and citizens were held hostage for 444 days at the U.S. Embassy in Tehran. ABC's nightly coverage of the hostage situation would become a late-night news program called "Nightline".) Plus, I never pass up a lunch at 13 Coins on somebody else's dime. As Dunkel held court at a large table at the restaurant, he described how the new 6:30 news show called "Top Story" would be like a local version of "Nightline." We would take the day's top local news story and explore it for twenty minutes, ending the program with a commentary, arts review or other "kicker." It would also be a showcase for longer-form news investigations. I was pretty psyched to become a reporter and co-anchor for the new show, joining Seattle veteran Mike James at the anchor desk.

And as it turned out, my ethnicity was exactly what Dunkel was looking for. In his book, *McGruff the News Hound*, Sandifer wrote:

"He (Dunkel) says, 'Now, we need another anchor, a woman. An Asian woman if possible.' Noticing my eyebrows go up he continues, 'They are little ratings getters; men love them, women aren't threatened by them, and they just get ratings. You know anybody like that?'

"'Lori Matsukawa, at KOMO,' I say. 'She's a former Miss America Teenager, just your cup of tea. She's cute, smart, a good reporter and I think I can get her over here.' We call her on the spot. She's in Olympia, the state capitol, holding down the KOMO bureau. She will come.'"

My first months at "Top Story" held both agony and ecstasy. Agony because I was intimidated by being plopped in a nest of well established, independent-minded mostly male journalists who "McGruff" was supposed to lasso into a manageable team each night.

`The "Top Story" reporters included Don McGaffin, Bob Simmons, Greg Palmer, Jim Compton and Mike James. They represented a type of news reporting that was unique to KING, an almost intellectual approach to and delivery of stories that was more commentary than reportage at times. This had been KING's signature style since the station arrived on Seattle airwaves in 1948. I was the newbie barging into a longstanding white men's club. But viewer tastes were changing; they wanted more and shorter stories in their newscasts. So news director Don Dunkel launched his experiment. Make the five o'clock and eleven o'clock newscasts more rapid-fire and the 6:30 p.m. program more pedantic with visually robust stories longer than four to five minutes. A local version of "Nightline." At any rate, it would be a good receptacle for Don McGaffin's hard crime investigations, Bob Simmons' national and international political analyses, Greg Palmer's theater and book reviews and Mike James' coverage of the Seattle Symphony. We also got great depth with the addition of Linda Brill from Chicago, Charlotte Raynor, KING's legislative reporter, Associate Producer John Wilson and researchers Ruth Pumphrey and Brian Redpath to our team.

The ecstasy happened when there was a decent "Top Story." The show was a fantastic showcase though it was sometimes a killer to gather, write and edit all the content needed. Remember, this was well before cheap satellite time, digital anything and cellphones. Political, health or environmental stories that needed more explanation and detail could "breathe" on Top Story. This was especially true when we covered stories such as the Challenger explosion, child sex abuse, the AIDs epidemic and the political divide between Eastern and Western Washington. It also gave me a platform to show some of my on-going coverage of the effort to attain redress for Japanese Americans who were incarcerated in American concentration camps during World War II. Seattle-area survivors of the camps were national leaders in the redress movement. There was also a very active Nisei Veterans Committee that wanted the history of their service members documented and shared with the public.

Learning about the television news business without a mentor to teach me the ropes was difficult. There was an unspoken pact in the city that every news station only needed one Asian anchor/reporter. I felt a huge obligation to work like heck to defend that reporting position and not let the Asian American community down. What some might call my "work ethic" was really me working every shift and weekend out of fear of being fired or replaced while I was away and couldn't defend that position.

Second, I had the notion that EVERYONE in the newsroom knew more about news reporting than I did. And while some people did know more, many others did not. This belief of mine made me lose out on the chance to cover meaty breaking news or pursue stories that required more than a day to research and report because I was too timid to fight for my idea. It took years for me to realize that I could do this job as well as or better than others in the newsroom. I just had to get in there and speak up.

And third, I was under the illusion that my hard work would "speak for itself" and that my managers would see how valuable I was to the team without me saying a thing. Was I ever wrong! I had to build up my courage for days before entering the news director's office to pitch a story or ask for a researcher's help. But I worked on it. I looked for opportunities to get into a casual conversation with news managers, producers and assignment editors so they could learn my interests and strengths without the stress of deadlines.

How great would it have been if there had been a mentor, male or female, who sat down and asked, "How's it going?" I could have used someone to share notes with and strategize about who and how to get stories done. I understand it is never part of anyone's job description. So when the chance to create a group that could do this appeared, I jumped in with both feet. It was called the Asian American Journalists Association, which would soon provide the support I needed and a way to help others navigate this industry run largely by white guys.

To its credit, KING proved to have an eye toward diversity even in the early Eighties. Hattie Kauffman, an indigenous (Nez Perce) woman anchored on the weekends. When she left to work for CBS, she was replaced by James Hattori, a Japanese American. Our news staff included African Americans Linda Kennedy and Lee Carter, Asian Americans Linda Taira, Cathy Kiyomura and Norm Ohashi. Over in programming there was Mimi Gan in "Evening" and Enrique Cerna, a Hispanic American who tapped me to co-host "Celebrate the Differences" with him, a show about the area's diverse neighborhoods and artists. And there were definitely women on air and in the management ranks.

Working with weeknight anchor Jean Enersen was a confounding experience. Yes, she was a pioneer in the business, being the first female weeknight evening news anchor in the country. Yes, she was inspiring other Seattle stations to hire women, but she was also a stone wall that I couldn't seem to get around.

News directors and station managers called her "The Franchise." KING was her first TV job out of Stanford and she never left. She didn't have to. In the Seventies, Eighties and Nineties, she held forth weeknights at five p.m., 6:30 p.m. and eleven p.m. getting first dibs on most of the plum stories and trips. KING's dominance in the ratings was largely attributed to Jean because she was well educated, blonde and wholesome and was on good terms with the Bullitt family who owned KING. She was a constant, even as the anchormen seated next to her changed often. Consultants said she appealed to the station's most desirable viewers: women twenty-five to forty-five (and in the early days, that meant white women).

We could only speculate that Jean made good money because by the time her contract was settled, the news managers said there wasn't a lot left for the rest of us to negotiate. I don't know that Jean had many newsroom buddies, the ones you had beers with or had over to the house. In fact, for the thirty-six years I worked at KING, Jean never invited me to a meal or to her home.

Still, there was more than enough work to go around. I was able to anchor several different newscasts and substitute for Jean over the years. And in such an ageist business as television, I felt as long as Jean was working, I was working!

Over time, I learned to temper my feelings about being the second banana. I remember walking past the lunchroom one day and seeing Jean huddled with Nancy Bergquist, the station's marketing manager.

"Harumph!" I thought to myself. "What big trip or story are they going to publicize now?" The very next day, I found out. They had been working on a news release about Jean's divorce from her husband, who came from a wealthy and influential family. At the time, their daughters were still young. I felt sorry for them and Jean having to reveal this personal news so publicly. What they say is true — things are not always as they seem.

CHAPTER 13
GOING TO THE "NET"

So, what's next for you?

Each time someone asked me this question, I replied, "I'd like to go to the 'Net,'" as in network news. At the time, I thought everyone in television news wanted to go to the network. Or at least a network O&O (owned and operated) station in a big city like New York or L.A. So here I was, in the late Eighties, early Nineties, anchoring the morning and weekend news shows after the demise of "Top Story." My reporting was challenging and interesting. I was able to pitch some major stories which (I thought) put me into network contention. Let's face it, as lovely as Seattle was, it was not considered the "Big Time." I wanted to prove to myself and others that Connie Chung wasn't the only Asian American woman who could work at the Net. I wanted to be able to sign off on stories saying, "Lori Matsukawa, NBC News, New York." "Lori Matsukawa, NBC News, Tokyo." "Lori Matsukawa, NBC News, London."

"I belong in the Big Time!" I told myself as I laser-focused on getting to the Net. The first step was getting a video reel together chock full of Net-level stories.

This obsession with the Net had driven me to support a new professional organization called the Asian American Journalists Association (AAJA). I needed a posse to help me get a Net job and this was the kind of group that could do that. And wouldn't you know it, it was created by my old college buddy, Bill Sing.

I was still at KOMO in 1983 when he took Larry and me to a Mexican restaurant to make his pitch. He wanted Seattle to be the third chapter of AAJA after Los Angeles and San Francisco. I was very interested in what Bill had to say. Here was the support group I never had working in the broadcast industry. Here was a group where I could find mentors and people who were looking to hire Asian American journalists. It was part of a "pipeline" that would feed talented Asian American journalists to the nation's newsrooms and perhaps the highest corporate offices. But I wanted to hear it from Bill.

"Why should I put out the effort?" I asked Sing over my burrito.

"Because we need to be visible. We need to be heard and hired. It's a lot easier when we're part of a big group," Sing explained.

"It would be nice to be in a big group like NABJ (the Black journalists)," I mused. "Newspaper and station managers flock to their convention to hire people. How wonderful would it be if we could advance our careers that way, you know, rub elbows with mucky mucks."

Sing had me hooked.

In the winter of 1984, Bill and AAJA Executive Director Karen Seriguchi (who had Seattle roots) met a bunch of us at the Dilettante Cafe on Capitol Hill. It was time to get organized.

There was Ron Chew, the editor of the International Examiner, an Asian American community newspaper; Frank Abe, a reporter at KIRO Newsradio (and, I would soon learn, a budding historian and documentary-maker) and Sharon Maeda, a Seattleite by birth who was executive director of Pacifica Radio in Los Angeles. A crazy bunch of people, for sure, but what we had in common was a shared commitment to accurate coverage of Asian American issues and communities, more hiring of Asian American journalists, advancement of Asian Americans once they were hired and inspiring the next generation of journalists through scholarships and mentorships.

We launched our chapter at the Bush Hotel in the International District on July 13, 1985. Both KABC anchor Tritia Toyota and Bill Sing were there at the kickoff, which attracted forty-five people. As AAJA's third chapter, we were catching what could be described as the minority employment wave sweeping the country as federal laws required media outlets to diversify in hiring as well as programming. Best of all, it felt good to be part of a larger movement. (As of 2020, AAJA had twenty-one chapters including one in Asia, with more than seventeen hundred members.)

For the first few years, we focused on networking with other journalists in town and at the national conventions. The Seattle Chapter held "Access to Media" workshops to teach community organizations how to pitch stories to television stations and newspapers. Seattle P-I editorial cartoonist David Horsey was so enthusiastic about AAJA's mission, he became a member (even though he's white) and drew the cover art for our workshop booklet. We held panels for members on investigative reporting, how to get fellowships and improving writing and speaking skills.

We had fun as well. We held a fundraiser dinner at the Space Needle in October 1992 with actor George Takei — Lt. Sulu of Star Trek fame. Yes, we shamelessly begged his niece, KING 5 sportscaster Akemi Takei, to invite him for us. George posed with each table of guests after uproariously cajoling them for a generous donation to the scholarship program. We also enjoyed monthly "Dim Sum Saturdays" that allowed us to meet new boyfriends, girlfriends, babies and folks from other chapters while enjoying cultural comfort food.

The biggest advantage of AAJA for me and countless journalists yet to come, was its national convention. Each year, several of us convinced our employers to pay for part or all of our costs to attend the AAJA National Convention. I attended the first one in Los Angeles in the fall of 1987 and couldn't believe my eyes. I was surrounded by hundreds of journalists from all across the country who looked like me! There was a job fair where more than thirty companies, from the *New York Times* to CBS, were actively trying to recruit and hire people. Media managers and producers donated their time to critique journalists' work, filing young journalists' resumes and demo reels into their briefcases as possible future hires. There was bonding and energy and networking. Some even met their future spouses at AAJA conventions. I'd always file a short report to my news director about what I learned and what a wonderful hiring opportunity AAJA conventions provided.

Seattle stations began moving away from the "single Asian" staffing model and started looking to fill slots with help from AAJA. In the late Eighties and well into the 2000s, Asian female broadcast journalists were hired more often than Asian men because they were "two-fers." They filled two affirmative action slots, being minority and female.

Those of us on television also benefited from the "Connie Effect." Connie Chung was a CBS network anchor at the time, so everyone in the entire nation knew who she was. Pretty much every Asian American female in television news was called "Connie" on the streets. At first, I tried to correct people, saying, "No, I'm Lori." But most just kept calling me Connie. "Great to see you, Connie!" Finally, I just gave up and would smile and wave when they shouted her name at me. I often thought to myself, "What would Connie Chung be doing at a 7-Eleven in Renton buying a pack of gum? It's ridiculous!" Years later, after I had been anchoring at KING for twenty or so years, my colleague Elisa Hahn said she went from being called Connie to being called Lori. Someone even asked her for an autograph.

"I signed it, L-O-R-I M-A-T-S-U-K-A-W-A with a flourish," Elisa laughed. So much for smashing the "All Asians look alike" myth.

Each year at the AAJA National Convention, I shopped my audition reel to network recruiters at the job fair. I felt self-conscious being in line with so many drop-dead gorgeous women clutching their own reels. I kept reminding myself that I was good enough. I was Net material. Several of us in the same situation compared notes over beers at the end of the day. "Should I hire an agent? Can you trust what so-and-so from network XYZ says? Can you make an introduction for me?" This was all precious intel.

Story selection for the reel became very important. What stories will resonate with recruiters? Are there enough shots of me participating in the piece? Is it a mix of live shots and recorded stories? One story I found particularly "Net-worthy" was about Edward Shige Yoshida, a Japanese Canadian man who was incarcerated during World War II. Here's how it came about. In 1991, the Canadian Consul in Seattle invited me to come to the tiny town of Chemainus, B.C. where they were going to dedicate a mural depicting Mr. Yoshida. While unjustifiably imprisoned with hundreds of Japanese families at the Vancouver Fairgrounds, Mr. Yoshida organized what would become the largest Boy Scout troop in North America.

"Yoshida himself will be coming from Ontario to Chemainus for the first time since the War to see it," smiled the consul.

This was screaming EPIC STORY to me, so I dashed to my news director. The good news? He let me off anchor duty Friday so I could travel to Chemainus and interview the artist. The bad news? I had to convince a photographer from "Evening" to make the arduous trip and return to anchor the 6:30 p.m. news Saturday because all the other anchors were on vacation. Videographer Ralph Bevins at "Evening" turned out to be a blessing. He was used to the artistic, long-form shooting this sort of story required. I didn't have to tell him about the sights and sounds I needed, because he already knew. The tight shot of artist Stanley Taniwa's brush, the closeup of Shige Yoshida's shoe as he stepped off the bus, the sonorous chanting of the Buddhist monk as incense smoke lifted into the air, the row of fresh-faced scouts standing at attention and a smiling Yoshida, wearing his vintage Boy Scout beret, soaking it all in. "This could definitely get me to the network!" I dreamed.

Indeed, I "sort of" made it to the Net by covering the 50th Anniversary of the attack on Pearl Harbor for NBC's Newchannel. I wrote feature stories, covered the ceremonies and did live shots for NBC affiliates all across the country. We got to Pearl Harbor before all the commemorative events began, so I got to introduce my photographer Bill Fenster and our editor Janet DiGangi to my folks. They lived right above Pearl Harbor in Aiea, so we popped in for some iced teas and took in the view of the Arizona Memorial. Mom got a little starry-eyed when she saw Fenster, who insisted on carrying his camera with him everywhere. It was as if she realized for the first time that her daughter really worked for a television station!

"Wanna see where we'll be working?" he asked with his Arizona charm. "It's just a news trailer on the base, but you're welcome to check it out."

"Can we?" asked Mom, all excited. Dad was an officer in the Army Reserve and said he had the decal on his car to drive right onto the base. No problem.

It was my first experience being the Newschannel live

shot reporter, so I was as excited as Mom and Dad about working elbow to elbow with the network crew.

The NBC Newschannel trailer coordinated all of the live shots for the affiliates and NBC Nightly News. The producers and photographers in that trailer were already eating their Thai takeout food since they were ALWAYS on East Coast time, five hours ahead of Hawaii. The NBC crew greeted Mom and Dad and went back to eating and editing and shouting out countdowns. I preferred the relative quiet of our affiliates' trailer, which we shared with the crew from KCRA Sacramento. I had pre-produced a couple of stories called "inserts" to be shown between my live open and close. One was a profile of a Port Orchard Medal of Honor recipient Captain Donald K. Ross who was going to introduce President George H.W. Bush at the Arizona Memorial. He received the medal for his heroic actions to save the USS Nevada during the attack on Pearl Harbor on December 7, 1941. The other insert was about a Japanese woman, living in Honolulu during the attack, whose young son died when a Japanese plane bombed their home.

On December 6 around noon, Fenster, the NBC field producer and I trotted to the pier to start our string of live shots. The producer dialed up the IFB communication to each station control room and told me the names of the anchors I'd be talking to. She cued me and I started talking. It was almost comical because I used the same toss to each station, only changing the names of the anchors. "Hello from Pearl Harbor, Cathy and Bob.... Hello from Pearl Harbor, Karen and Rick .... Hello from Pearl Harbor, Jerry and Monica ...." As evening arrived, Fenster had to light the battleship Missouri behind me. "Oh yeah, just light the entire freakin' battleship!" crowed Fenster, who loved a challenge. "Hello from Pearl Harbor, Barry and Jean ..."

The next morning, as President George H.W. Bush arrived for the Fiftieth Anniversary Ceremony, anti-war demonstrators started kicking up a fuss outside the Pearl Harbor main gate.

"I'll go get some footage," mumbled Fenster, as he grabbed his camera and left the trailer.

"I'll stay here and watch the feed of the president," I called after him. A short while later, the KCRA crew dashed into the trailer.

"Hey, your photographer got arrested!" reporter Gordon Tokumatsu shouted.

"What?? Don't bother me! The president is just about to talk!" I was busy writing down the timecode of the video feeding into our trailer.

"No seriously, he got put in a cop car!" exclaimed the photographer, shoving a videocassette into his machine. I stared in shock. There was Fenster, his hands cuffed behind his back, a police officer holding the top of his head and pushing him down into the back seat of a cruiser. There was some muffled shouting and the officer picked up Fenster's camera and tossed it into the back seat. The car drove off.

"Oh my God, where did they take him?" I shouted. The photographer shrugged. I knew the closest police station was in Pearl City, just west of Pearl Harbor. I called the first person I thought of … my mom!

As Fenster later recalled, he was trying to get a wide shot of the protesters and hustled across Nimitz Highway to the grass median.

"Eh, get off the road!" a husky Hawaiian in a black T-shirt and jeans yelled at him.

"Yeah, yeah," said Fenster. "Just let me get this shot." He figured his NBC News hat and logo on his camera would cut him some slack with this excited local.

"I said, 'Get off the road!'" yelled the T-shirted man, who turned out to be a plainclothes officer. He grabbed Fenster, dragging him across the highway, while trying to cuff him at the same time.

"Wait! Wait! Watch the camera!" Fenster yelled, as he laid the thirty-pound video camera on the grass. It was worth a small fortune.

The officer took Fenster to the Pearl City police station. Fenster said the police removed his shoelaces and put him in a holding cell with a man he described as a "huge Samoan guy from an alternative lifestyle." The Samoan guy asked sweetly, "What you in for?"

Fenster said he growled back, "They said I killed somebody."

Fenster held back his laughter as the Samoan guy's eyes got wide and he moved away from that "dangerous *Haole*."

"I was napping in my cell," Fenster continued, "when suddenly I heard someone screaming, "Is THIS how we treat visitors to our community??"

It was my mom! She had driven down to the sub-station and was yelling at the police commander. Soon, an officer let Fenster out of the cell. The commander apologized for the incident but still gave him a ticket for jaywalking.

Fenster said when he was at the airport preparing to leave Hawai'i, he saw a newspaper with a photo of him in handcuffs. The story said it was the only problem police had during the three-day commemoration. A woman came up to him and pointed at the newspaper and said, "You da guy!"

Fenster beamed, "I was so proud."

Unbeknownst to me back at KING, News Director Bob Jordan was fighting a war of his own. He told me before I left that I was the obvious choice to cover the story because I grew up in Hawai'i and could use my contacts to get some unique stories. And he said it made sense that I do the NBC Newschannel live shots since I was good at thinking on my feet and could answer almost any questions the anchors at the other stations could throw at me.

When my reports hit the air, KING got flooded with calls.

Who's that Jap reporter covering the Pearl Harbor story? My uncle was killed in the war! I'm not going to watch KING anymore! etc.

My newsroom colleagues said Jordan went ballistic. "This is 1991!" he bellowed. He personally began taking calls at the desk defending me. I thanked him when I heard what he did. I was grateful my boss stood up for me.

"F-----g idiots," he growled.

FOR SEVERAL SUMMERS in the late Eighties and early Nineties, I made my rounds at the Asian American Journalists Association Convention Job Fair, pitching my video reel and jockeying for that network job offer. It didn't come. I kept adding anchoring highlights and "network level" live shots to my reel like coverage of President Clinton and Chinese President Jiang Zemin at the Asia Pacific Economic Cooperation on Blake Island in 1993. Crickets.

And then one momentous day in 1993, I received THE call. Elena Nachmanoff was hired by NBC in 1990 to recruit talent for the network. She was a former agent at N.S. Bienstock, a New York-based talent agency, which coincidentally had done publicity for the Miss Teenage America pageant way back when! She was recruiting at all the minority journalist conventions at the time. I remember telling her, summer after summer, how I wanted to be able to say: Lori Matsukawa, NBC News, Tokyo. Lori Matsukawa, NBC News, London. Lori Matsukawa, NBC News, New York.

Elena's voice was cheerful. "We have an opening for a correspondent based in L.A.," she started. My heart was beating fast. "Your beat would be covering the Western states for NBC Nightly News with Tom Brokaw." I almost passed out. She may have said something about starting at the base correspondent's salary, but I didn't remember anything past "Tom Brokaw." And then, "You'll need to live in L.A. and start soon. Let me know by the end of the week."

The offer that should have been a "no brainer" suddenly got difficult. You see, during all those years I was trolling for a network job, I was also living my life! I was active in organizations, emceeing their events and serving on a few boards. Larry and I had a son, Alex, born in 1987. We had a Golden retriever named Bo. Larry was climbing the management ladder at the local ABC affiliate. By the time Elena called, Alex, was six and thriving as a first grader at Cougar Ridge Elementary. Larry and I helped launch the after-school care program there, so Alex could play with his buddies until one of us picked him up after work.

Larry and I considered the possibilities: We could become a two-city family with me living in L.A. and Larry and Alex staying in Washington state. Well, what's the point of that? Not to mention it would be exhausting. Or Larry could quit his job, and our family could make a new home in L.A. Living in L.A. suddenly became an issue for me. Was it fair to Larry and Alex to pick up and transport themselves to another place? Especially since Larry had spent the last eighteen years climbing up the career ladder with excellent prospects ahead. My job as a correspondent would mean I could be ANYWHERE on any day, not just along the West Coast but in Las Vegas, Vancouver B.C. or Denver! I couldn't guarantee I'd be able to pick up Alex at his after-school daycare. In fact, Alex would probably not attend a public school close to home like he was doing now. That would be expensive. And where could we afford to live and what sort of commute would that require? As it was now, we were twenty minutes from the office to home.

I fretted. I fumed. Why is this decision so hard? Larry was sympathetic.

"Lori, what do YOU want? Whatever it is, we can make it work," he told me.

What DID I want?

"I want to say, 'Lori Matsukawa, NBC News, Beijing,'" I

whined. But in reality, I knew a West Coast correspondent would more likely be saying "Lori Matsukawa, NBC News, Long Beach, Oakland or … God forbid … Portland!"

In the end, I told Elena "no" because I just couldn't see raising a family in Los Angeles. I chose family over career. I had a mini wake in my heart, mourning the death of a long-held dream.

But then, the most astonishing thing happened. KING TV began sending me to cover stories in amazing places. I covered the arrival of Washington state apples in Japan for the first time in twenty-five years. I also did other business/trade stories about Washington products. I really got to say, "Lori Matsukawa KING 5 News, Tokyo" and "KING 5 News, Sendai", too! There was an earthquake and military airlift to Nicaragua. "Lori Matsukawa, KING 5 News, Managua." I covered the New Hampshire Primaries and Iowa Caucuses in 2000 focusing on John McCain and George W. Bush. In the ladies' room, I was washing hands and exchanging pleasantries with the very NBC correspondents whom I had envied in the past! "Lori Matsukawa, KING 5 News, Concord, New Hampshire." "Lori Matsukawa, KING 5 News, Des Moines, Iowa." The 2002 Winter Olympics were held in Salt Lake City. I got to cover an emerging short-track skating star named Apolo Ohno from Federal Way, Washington. "Lori Matsukawa, KING 5 News, at the Winter Olympic Games, Salt Lake City." A monument to Japanese American incarceration camp survivors was dedicated at the nation's capital. "Lori Matsukawa, KING 5 News, Washington." A huge highlight of my career was covering Washington Governor Gary Locke's first trade mission to China where he met then-President Jiang Zemin. "Lori Matsukawa, KING 5 News, Beijing, Hong Kong, Shanghai, Guangzhou, Chengdu." And as a "local news" reporter, I did things "Net" correspondents didn't normally do — like pull nine Gs in an F-16 Thunderbird or apply lipstick before my live shot in the dugout at Yankee Stadium as the Seattle Mariners took a shot at an American League Championship. "Lori Matsukawa, KING 5 News, New York." It was my "Net" dream come true and I didn't have to leave my Seattle home. Larry and Alex were happy for me and got some really cool souvenirs over the years.

CHAPTER 14

MAKE THE BIG TIME
WHERE YOU ARE

Make the Big Time Where You Are.

That's what coach Forrest Edward "Frosty" Westering always told his players and coaches. The beloved Pacific Lutheran University head coach knew most folks would not consider playing PLU football in Tacoma, Washington, to be the "Big Time" … unless you made it so. The wise coach taught that what's going on right where you are MATTERS.

So, with my Net obsession put to rest, I decided to pivot. I would now focus my energy on being my best self right where I was — in Seattle. I could strive to be a more effective reporter and anchor, a more engaged wife and mom and a mentor to aspiring journalists. It was a great feeling. And should the Net come calling one day, that would be icing on the cake.

Job one was to make Seattle a "Big Time" place using AAJA as a vehicle. Our chapter had already dipped a toe into this area a few years earlier by hosting a national AAJA Convention in 1991. Although our attendance was smaller than New York's (fewer than five hundred compared to a record 750) we had several firsts that became standard at future conventions such as Student Pizza Night, an ethnic media mini-convention, single-day workshops for skill building and "Project Zinger," a compilation of the year's worst coverage of Asian American issues and communities.

We had James Hattori, who left KING in 1987 for Houston before landing at CBS, and Gary Matsumoto, a foreign correspondent at NBC news keynote our gala. They talked about their experiences covering the Persian Gulf War. I was proud we invited them because they were part of an elite group — Asian American *male* broadcasters. There were (and still are!) so few Asian American men on television. They are the minority within the minority. AAJA even published two "Men of AAJA" calendars to raise awareness about their lack of representation. In an interview with the AAJA Convention newspaper *Voices* in August 2014, George Kiriyama said a lot of it is due to a lack of role models and often family pressure on sons to pursue high-paying, stereotypically Asian American jobs — doctor, dentist, engineer. Kiriyama, who used to be an on-air reporter before being promoted to managing editor at KTNV in Las Vegas, says his hope was that the calendars would attract more Asian American men into the industry.

The Seattle Chapter also hosted a Unity convention in 1999. Unity was a once-every-four-years convention of four journalists of color organizations: the Asian American Journalists Association, the National Association of Black Journalists (NABJ), the National Association of Hispanic Journalists (NAHJ) and the Native American Journalists Association (as of 2023 the Indigenous Journalists Association). An estimated six thousand people attended but I'll always remember it as the time GOP presidential candidate George W. Bush did the "drive-by handshake" as he came down the escalator at the State Convention Center. He was in Seattle for a campaign stop and hadn't even thought to check out what all these journalists of color were doing in town. An article about the convention written by Sam Fulwood III for the *Los Angeles Times* convinced Bush's staff that he should at least cruise through the crowds!

A note about Unity: Journalists of Color, later to be called Unity: Journalists of Diversity. The coalition was created in 1990 as a way for organizations representing journalists of color to collaboratively meet common goals such as coverage of minority issues and hiring and promoting journalists of color. Unity Conventions were held in Atlanta (1994), Seattle (1999), Washington, D.C. (2004), Chicago (2008) and Las Vegas (2012). I particularly enjoyed the convention in Chicago because we were addressed by then-Senator Barack Obama who had the audacity to run for (and become) America's first Black president. However, lack of funding and differing priorities doomed the organization. Unity officially closed in February 2018.

A proud moment for our chapter was posthumously nominating Walt and Milly Woodward, publishers of the *Bainbridge Review,* for a national AAJA Special Recognition Award. The Woodwards were the only newspaper publishers on the West Coast to speak out against Executive Order 9066, which forced 120,000 people of Japanese ancestry into American concentration camps during World War II. The Woodwards declared the order was unconstitutional and morally wrong. They suffered a loss of advertising and sales as a result of their stance. A sizable number of Japanese American Bainbridge Islanders were forced to leave their homes and businesses in March of 1942. Before they boarded the ferries to Seattle and beyond, Walt appointed four young people as "internment camp correspondents" to send missives back to the newspaper. Walt wanted to know about births, deaths, marriages and baseball scores because he felt the Japanese Americans "are our neighbors" and he wanted to keep in touch until they returned home. The award was accepted at the AAJA National Convention in San Francisco in 2001 by

Paul Ohtaki, one of the "camp correspondents." In August 2001, Ohtaki told the *Kitsap Sun,* "Knowing the Woodwards, I think they'd be very honored. They'd be happy to know the fact they stood up for the Japanese Americans and the Constitution of the United States is being recognized."

AAJA Seattle Chapter Co-President Phong Le and I later presented the award to Mary Woodward, Walt and Milly's daughter, at a Bainbridge Island City Council meeting. The *Kitsap Sun* quoted me, saying, "One of the biggest regrets of my life is that I never got a chance to meet him (Walt) and thank him for being courageous. They (Walt and Milly) did what a lot of people felt in their hearts, and for that the Japanese American community is eternally grateful." Mary was quoted as saying, "They would both be very humbled. Partly, because at the time, they didn't feel they were on a crusade, they just felt they were doing what was right."

Despite the Seattle Chapter's growing visibility, the hiring of Asian American hiring in print, broadcast, digital and photography was slow. Each time I asked a local news director about hiring more Asian American journalists, the most common reaction was, "I'd hire an Asian American journalist, but where do I find one?" It was obvious that we had to "prime the pump" — get young people into the journalism pipeline so we could point to them and say, "There they are!" The best way to get that pipeline going was to award scholarships so that aspiring journalists of color could go to college, stay in college and find journalism jobs and mentors when they got out.

In 1986, the recipient of AAJA Seattle's first scholarship was Judy Averill who got $250 that the journalists dug out of their pockets at the reception. To her credit, the University of Washington student went on to become a reporter and editor at the *Seattle Times.* Over the years, AAJA Seattle and NABJ Seattle combined forces to create the Northwest Journalists of Color (NJC) Scholarship program. As of 2020, NJC had presented nearly a hundred students with close to $250,000. The news directors and publishers donated to the scholarship program because we told them we were "priming the pump" for them. Our scholarship winners went on to write for big newspapers, magazines, work at television and radio stations and become news photographers and digital editors. Some left journalism for jobs in law, social work or teaching. Others work in tech or serve as marketing and diversity consultants. No matter. We simply wanted to support the students and help them realize the Big Time was what they made it.

AAJA, and the scholarship program in particular, was a wonderful vehicle for me to develop leadership skills and get to know the news directors, editors and publishers in town. I felt I had a certain "entree" and that I could "sit at the table" to discuss issues such as diversity in hiring and coverage of minority communities as a peer, rather than an underling. And there's no greater leadership skill than being able to raise money for a cause. After two AAJA conventions and two decades of awarding scholarships, I felt very comfortable asking for dough.

Two men who modeled leadership for me were Frank Blethen, the publisher of the family-owned *Seattle Times* and his then-managing editor, Alex MacLeod. When I went to them for scholarship donations, they greeted me generously. They never said "no" or waved me away, although now that I think about it, they could have easily done so. They were just straight shooters who believed firmly in racial diversity.

"You can't report on your community if you don't have reporters from the community," was Alex's bottom line. Alex attended several AAJA conventions and headed recruitment at the *Seattle Times* job fair booth for at least a decade. He or Frank (and in later years, Executive Editor David Boardman) always took the Seattle chapter attendees out for a big meal in the convention city. The *Times* managers often attended Seattle chapter activities like the Lunar New Year Banquet and scholarship reception. For two years, beginning in 2008, the company paid travel expenses and allowed time off to *Times* reporter Sharon Pian Chan to serve as National AAJA president during what Chan described as "a time of utmost financial duress" at the newspaper.

This kind of leadership was not lost on other chapter members. The scholarship program got a huge boost in 2004 when Sharon, Robert Hernandez (a member of NAHJ) and Michael Ko — all journalists at the *Seattle Times* — got together for beers and tacos at Bluwater Bistro after work. "Why don't we raise money for an endowment?" Sharon asked. "That way, we don't have to keep begging for money from the newspapers and stations every year and the program would be self-sustaining." They decided to make an endowment appeal straight to individuals and chapter members in addition to the major publishers and broadcasters in town. The three of them co-chaired the campaign for two years, then handed over the reins to Sanjay Bhatt (*Seattle Times*) and Susan Han (KCTS). The goal was to raise a hundred thousand dollars in five years — they raised it in four!

"This is what it means to be in the Big Time!" I thought as I mentally crossed off donation visits to the city's publishers and news directors for the foreseeable future. I realized many individuals contributing in one way or another, big or small, were making Seattle a desirable place to live and work, at least in my opinion. And yes, the number of Asian American journalists kept increasing in the 2000s. AAJA was the pipeline so many of us had envisioned. To keep it going, I dedicated myself to teaching our student scholarship winners how to "work the convention" and incorporate it into their professional lives.

I gathered the students just before the convention for a "tutorial." Following the lead of my mentors at the *Seattle Times*, my husband and I often took them out to dinner to impart this "wisdom" and let them know how proud we were of them.

"It's important to get your posse together," I told Brady Wakayama from Washington State University. "All you first-time student convention go-ers need to stick together and experience the convention as a group. These people will become your AAJA cohort. These are the people you will commiserate with, swap stories with and reconnect with at every subsequent convention your entire careers. When someone in AAJA is being promoted to a bigger market, they will call you and tell you to apply for their old job. If you are leaving your market for a better job, you will reach out to your cohort and reach back to those behind you and encourage them to apply for *your* old job. This chain will continue to pull Asian American journalists up through the ranks and possibly into management. Take advantage of this resource, because it didn't exist when I first left college. This organization will take you far .... if you let it." In 2005, I received an AAJA Lifetime Achievement Award due, in part, to my undying confidence in these aspiring journalists of color.

CHAPTER 15
THE LOCKE CONNECTION

"Can you invite Mona over to our place for dinner? We'd like her to meet Gary."

I had never been part of setting up a blind date before. But here was Benson Wong trying to get me to invite my news colleague to his home to meet a guy! I met Benson, a local attorney, doing reports on efforts to clear the U.S. Supreme Court record of wartime curfew resister Gordon Hirabayashi. The "guy" he was trying to introduce was Gary Locke, the legislator I met nine years earlier in Olympia. Turns out, he was also Benson's former brother-in-law.

At the time (about 1992), Gary was working in the private sector as well as the state legislature and contemplating a run for King County executive. He was fourteen years older than Mona Lee, who was a new reporter at KING, fresh out of Green Bay, WI, who sat at the desk just over the divider from me. Mona and a bunch of us at KING knew each other through the Asian American Journalists Association.

To my surprise, Mona said she was open to dinner. It did not go well.

First of all, getting to Benson's house was a nightmare. Mona followed Larry and me in her car. When I stopped on the side of the driveway and opened my door, it scraped Mona's car door as she was driving past! Then there was the slightly awkward introduction. Mona, Gary. Gary, Mona. "So, what do you think of politicians?" he asked. "Not much," she replied. I felt totally deflated during the dinner, though it appeared my husband and Mona had a really lively conversation the whole time. I did suggest Gary run for King County executive. "How else can you become governor??" I teased as Larry, Mona and I made our way out.

I was pretty glum after that episode. Larry told me to cheer up. "These things don't often pan out."

Not long after that, Larry and I went to see "Phantom of the Opera" at the Fifth Avenue Theater when, all of a sudden, I caught a glimpse of Gary and Mona walking toward their seats across the floor. I clutched Larry's arm. "They're dating!" I gasped.

"Ouch. What? Oh…!" was Larry's reply.

So I was pretty happy knowing things were indeed working out. In early 1993, our newsroom became the battleground for what I called "The War of the Roses." Gary was courting Mona by sending a dozen roses to the office each month. Turns out, Mona had a couple of other suitors, and THEY sent roses to the office as well.

"This is getting weird!" I shouted into the rose bouquet hedge that was suddenly blocking my view of Mona's desk.

"What am I going to do?" her voice came back.

"Umm, make up your mind?" I suggested.

After a ridiculous number of bouquets lived and died on her desk, I received a rose in a bud vase delivered to my desk. Gary had popped the question — something involving a plane pulling a banner. In the fall of 1993, Gary was elected King County executive. Their wedding was in October 1994. But I didn't attend their California wedding because I believed I couldn't take time off anchoring the weekend news to attend. I was going to protect that anchor chair like a

Mama Bear. No one could accuse me of slacking on the job, no sir. This was proof that I had a work ethic that wouldn't quit. It was also one of the dumbest decisions of my life.

Decades later, in 2016, out-going Vice President Joe Biden was in Seattle touring Fred Hutchinson Cancer Research Center as part of his "Cancer Moonshot" tour. As we were getting ready to do our one-on-one interview, I mentioned that I helped Gary and Mona get together. The vice president knew Gary well, as he had served as secretary of commerce and ambassador to China in the Obama administration by then. Vice President Biden bent his head close and smiled: "Gary and I, we both married up!"

One of the advantages of playing matchmaker to a future governor is when the governor goes to China, you have a good chance of going with him! When I got wind in 1997 of Governor Gary Locke's first trade mission to China with a side trip to his ancestral village, I immediately called his press office to put KING's hat in the press corps ring. Then came what I thought would be the hard part, convincing our news director Eric Lerner to let me and a videographer go along.

The pitch went surprisingly well. I started ticking through the pluses. He's the first Chinese American governor. This is his first trade mission on behalf of the state of Washington. China is Washington's second largest trading partner. He's going to his ancestral village for the first time and his dad is going along with him. His entourage will include representatives from Washington agriculture, banking and business including wheat and apple farmers and folks from Microsoft and the University of Washington School of Business. We would be the only local television crew. Eric's eyes lit up. BINGO!

It was going to cost KING a small sum plus the newsroom would be down a weeknight anchor during this ten-day sojourn, but that was Eric Lerner's problem, not mine. I was happy videographer Dave Wike agreed to go with me. We had good chemistry and I knew he was a hard worker. Plus, he was tall and that proved to be an advantage when we began plowing into the unbelievable crush of Chinese who wanted to see the first Chinese American governor.

When we got to Beijing, the first thing on the governor's agenda was barreling along the Great Wall. For some reason, Gary seemed determined NOT to be photographed by Dave and me. He scurried ahead of us, so we only got shots of his receding back and his security entourage. It's not like we didn't try to get ahead of him for an approach shot, but the steps on the wall were steep, some two to two and a half feet high! I was carrying Dave's wooden tripod so he could grab shots off his shoulder as we quickly lost sight of the governor. We were furious with him because while he was up ahead, he flew a Chinese kite above the wall which was captured by *Seattle Times* photographer, Rod Mar. Meanwhile, Dave and I were so far behind, we decided to stay put and catch the governor on his way back. We recorded a few stand-ups I had hurriedly written in the van ride to the wall. We then took a seat above a narrow stairwell to wait. And … suddenly … everything … went white. The next thing I heard was, "Is she alright? Does she need some water?"

Dave said I fainted and slipped to the stone floor in a sitting position.

"Mats!" he yelped and kept his hand behind my back. Thank goodness he did, because if I had fainted backward, I would have plunged fifteen feet down the stone stairway. I guess the altitude and running with a heavy tripod after getting off a plane was too much for me. Suddenly, I saw the entourage coming back toward us. No time for sympathy! Dave and I hurried over to get the video we needed of the governor coming down toward us.

"Governor, you've got to work with me," I pleaded. (It was strange calling him "governor" all the time, considering he was Mona's husband and therefore a friend. But this was, after all, a professional trip!)

"Oh, sorry about that," Gary said when told about the fainting episode. Thus began the first day of "Lori and Dave's TV news video training" for the governor, which would ultimately serve him well in the years to come. These are the basic rules if you ever find yourself being taped for a news story. During an interview, stop, pause and start again if you stumble on a thought or sentence. Look the interviewer in the eye and speak plainly and simply. After the interview, stay put so the videographer can grab a two-shot (exactly what it sounds like, a shot of you and the interviewer) and some cutaways or reverse shots (shots of the back of your head, your eyes, your face listening and a shot over your shoulder showing the interviewer listening to you). There's the ever-popular "walking two shot" where you and the interviewer walk together toward the camera, past the camera and away from the camera. During our tour of the Forbidden City, Gary and I did a slightly more complicated move — looking at the ornately decorated pavilions and commenting on them at the same time! This was a great way to show the governor's real-time reaction as he encountered China's Imperial artifacts. What looked like an easy-going tour of the palace compound was really a complex shoot that Dave and I had discussed that morning at breakfast. He told me the visual and audio elements he needed to tell today's story. I had pre-written parts I planned to use within the story during the bus ride over. I also wrote "teases" and "promotions." These recorded snippets would be used by the news producers to set up my story within their newscasts and going into commercial breaks. Every shot and element had to be unique, interesting and help the viewer experience what the governor was experiencing. And we had to keep up with the entourage! There was a lot of pressure to do the teases in one take, because there was no time for do-overs.

Dave and I were pretty much working twelve to fifteen hour days, as the governor's handlers had each day packed with meetings and events. When the rest of the entourage went out for lunch, Dave and I hit the city to get video we needed to tell our stories. The obvious image: hordes of people, many of them riding bicycles through the streets and side alleys of Beijing. (Remember this was back in 1997). These were the potential consumers of Washington state products. We videotaped a vendor making noodles by hand. Was he using Washington grown white wheat? We found crates of apples bearing a Washington state seal, but we weren't sure if they were authentic. Dave got up early in the morning to grab images of the sun rising above a tiled temple roof and crowds of senior citizens doing Tai Chi in the park. I peeled away members of the entourage to do interviews about their area of interest. The agriculture rep wanted to talk about apples, cherries and wheat. The education rep wanted to talk about research and student exchanges. The timber folks wanted to convince China to import finished products as opposed to raw logs. We repeated this in city after city. In Shanghai we toured the shopping district to see how Microsoft products were being marketed. Dave and I climbed up bamboo scaffolding (which would never pass muster in the States) to observe the construction of a joint-venture manufacturing complex. We toured Shanghai's Bund (historic international settlement) at night to contrast its nineteenth century buildings to the super modern ones emerging across the river in Pudong. In Cheng Du, we toured a market that was selling Washington state potato chips. The market's manager obligingly put on a KING TV cap. Next stop, a school where the boys were playing basketball. "Michael Jordan!" I yelled as a youngster made a basket. "Oooh!" they crowed. They knew who HE was. Somewhere along the way, we did a stand-up on a Boeing aircraft.

Everywhere we went, crowds pressed around Locke and his entourage. It was exhausting. Why the fuss?

"He's the first Chinese American governor," explained Connie Wong, vice president of Nextel's business development in Asia. "It is like their Little Brother has come home. They are so proud of him."

Dave was fortunate enough to go to the governor's meeting with President Jiang Zemin. They only allowed photographers to attend the ceremonial handshaking. Gary later told me it was the biggest honor of his trip, hands down. President Jiang had echoed Connie Wong's sentiments: China was proud to welcome home an honored Chinese American leader.

During the evening hours while the entourage was having dinner or enjoying a cultural show, Dave and I made our way to the NBC Bureau to edit our stories. Our plan was to satellite the stories from the first part of the trip back to KING in one fell swoop so they could start broadcasting them, then personally bring back the stories from the second half of the trip — including Gary's visit to his ancestral village — to edit in Seattle.

Sending our stories by satellite to KING from the CCTV center was straight out of a spy novel. It was about eight p.m. The NBC van drove up to a solid timber gate. Our guide was the NBC bureau chief, a young blond fellow. He jumped out of the van and shouted at the dark gate in Mandarin.

SWOOSH. A mail slot door slid open. Two dark eyes peered out at us.

"Put your passports in there," the bureau chief ordered.

Dave and I did as we were told. I prayed I would see mine again.

SWOOSH. The slot door closed. We waited.

Slowly, the timber gate began to open. Our van drove through and up to a modern skyscraper. The CCTV building.

Dave, the bureau chief and I hopped out and entered. Our

shoes echoed on the marble floor. The hallway was dimly lit along the walls. We saw shadowy guards holding assault rifles spaced every so many feet on either side of us. The bureau chief took us up the elevator. When the doors opened, we were relieved. This hallway was lit! We walked into a room with stacks of Beta cassette machines. We grinned. This looked familiar! In fact, the engineer looked like a KING engineer. He wore blue jeans, a Rugby-type shirt and running shoes. Dave gave him the satellite coordinates and while he set them up, I dialed the KING engineer in Seattle, where it was early morning. The cellphone I was using was one of those brick-sized Motorola models. The phone connection was crappy. I told Torgy on the other end of the line to hang on while I went to a better spot. I wandered down the hall and into a dark room that had open windows.

"Do you hear me now?" I hollered.

"Hear you just fine," said Torgy. "I'm rolling."

I smiled. I could hear the audio of our stories in the background over the phone.

"It's working!" I thought. As my eyes adjusted to the darkness, my smile slowly faded. The dark room with the windows turned out to be a men's restroom. "Oh please, don't let any of those scary soldiers with guns come in now!" I prayed. The minutes ticked by. All the stories were fed.

"I got 'em all. Looks like you and Dave are getting a lot done!" said Torgy.

I thanked him and literally ran out of the restroom. Dave, the bureau chief and I left the building. I didn't even look at the men with guns as I hurried out the door into the night. We drove back out the timbered gate. Stopped the van. The mysterious mail slot door swished open. Our passports emerged. I grabbed them as the door slid shut.

The mystery of CCTV gave way to mayhem in the Locke ancestral village. Jilong is in Guangdong Province. We boarded a Jetfoil in Hong Kong with Gary and Mona, Gary's parents, siblings and the Washington press corps. It was Gary's first visit to the village that his great-grandfather left in the late 1800s to work on the railroads in the United States. His grandfather left the village in the 1930s, bringing along Gary's father Jimmy as a teenager. Gary's grandfather worked as a houseboy in Olympia, Washington, where he washed dishes and swept floors a mile from the governor's mansion. Gary joked that it took his family a hundred years to travel that one mile.

As the Jetfoil chopped through the water, the family members busied themselves putting money into red envelopes called *lai see* or "lucky money." These were for the hordes of relatives and hangers-on who were expected to greet the family as they arrived in the village. In the villagers' eyes, the Lockes were successful Chinese coming home from *Gam Saan* — "Gold Mountain" — America. Dave and I watched the shoreline whiz by. The tall grassy fields probably hadn't changed in two hundred years.

We disembarked near the city of Taishan, and it was pandemonium! Photographers and hordes of people pushed against iron railings on either side of the gangplank leading to the waiting motorcade. Everyone wanted to see the first Chinese American governor. He was a rock star!

Gary and Mona were surprised by the crowd and started doing a celebrity wave or two. They were supposed to attend a luncheon with the mayor of Taishan before heading to the village. The shouting and camera flashes filled the hot, steamy air. Alarmingly, the metal railings ended and the crowd pressed in. A couple dozen police officers had to join hands and form a human chain to keep the fans from swallowing Gary and Mona! From then on, all we saw were people. People lined alongside the road, people waving and smiling and people selling snacks. A brass band with students in red military style uniforms added to the din outside the mayor's office.

It was a relief to pile back into our minibuses and head to the village.

During the hour-long drive, I jotted down notes I had gleaned from conversations with Gary and his father, Jimmy. In preparation for the visit, the village had purchased a porcelain toilet, but since there was no indoor plumbing, it was simply placed in Eldest Uncle's house for show. The tiny brick houses had little or no electricity. Fortunately, Eldest Uncle's house had a single bulb hanging by a cord, so we MIGHT get a shot of the family altar plastered with photographs of Gary and his father. There was a quarter-acre fish pond in front of the village. Once a year, it was drained and the fattened fish sold at the market, the proceeds split among all the villagers.

The buses turned off the highway onto a dusty dirt road that ran through a rice field. Along the road were an estimated thousand youth waving pom poms and streamers, beating drums and marching in place in wing-like costumes. There were at least four brass bands. Scattered between them were young boys clanging cymbals and beating small drums. Curious farmers, moms with babies and various onlookers gawked. Finally, a white adobe wall came into view. We had arrived at Jilong.

Firecrackers started crackling. Sparks and the smell of gunpowder filled the air. Drums, gongs, lion dancers and a hundred or so residents greeted the Lockes, who had brought so much honor to their village.

"Ah, when I was a boy, this is where I waited for my grandfather to come home and bring me candy," said Jimmy Locke nostalgically.

A bouquet of flowers was thrust into Mona's arms as she and Gary proceeded into the narrow walkways of the village. They were sandwiched — front and back — by a horde of press photographers from Hong Kong and Beijing. The shouting and ruckus were incredible. Dave and I were pushed along by sweaty bodies. Again, Dave's height gave him an advantage getting video, but there was so much pushing and shoving it was pretty shaky stuff.

"Wow, everything is so old," observed Mona, who as a former television news reporter was conscious of the microphones all around them.

"So old and unchanged from a hundred years ago," added Gary, taking his cue.

When the Locke family ducked into an uncle's home, the press horde was kept out. That didn't stop photographers from standing on their gear bags (or each other) to take pictures through the upper windows. Inside an uncle's living room, Gary and his father admired photos and a Gary Locke campaign poster on the wall. I noticed Gary's security detail looking nervously at the scrum of photographers outside shouting the Chinese version of "Governor, look here!"

At the village cemetery, the Locke family members were allowed some space to place incense and a roast piglet as offerings at the family gravesite. Space, but not quiet. There was still a lot of hollering and confusing gestures that either meant "Come here!" or "Go away!" It was hard to tell.

Despite the commotion around me, I had to chuckle. This was the excitement of a Miss Teenage America parade times a thousand! The cheers and waves from total strangers. Crowds pressing close to catch a glimpse of fellow Chinese returning from America. I felt people were connecting, if only for an instant. The people we met in the village and throughout our journey were so proud of what Gary had accomplished.

"Would people in Japan be equally proud of their ancestors who went to the United States and returned?" I wondered. "Do they even *know* our history?" I doubted it. Gone and forgotten. That was the fate of my grandparents and every Japanese immigrant who left Japan. If such a time came, I wanted to be part of the remembering. I wanted to tell their story, just as Gary's visit was adding to the history of Jilong village.

"Goodbye and thank you for bringing such honor to our village," effused the villagers as we all clambered onto the buses.

"That was pretty amazing," groaned Dave as he finally took a seat.

Months after our return from China, the governor's office gave all the press corps T-shirts that read, "I Survived Jilong Village."

CHAPTER 16
PROMOTION/DEMOTION

Sixteen months. That's all it took to reach a career high and then slam into a career wall. Was the hard work I'd been putting in all for naught? Was institutional racism and racial stereotyping coming to wreak havoc on my career? From 1998 to 1999, I still believed in merit-based promotions, even in the fickle television news business. I naively thought my reporting chops, such as the Governor Locke China exclusive and good ratings, would someday be rewarded with an anchor assignment on a weeknight news program.

Not that I didn't appreciate anchoring the weekend newscasts. Having days off during the week allowed me to attend graduate school at the University of Washington for a year to earn a master's degree in communication in 1996. I was still trying to stick to my original plan hatched in that Redding Greyhound station to be a print reporter or perhaps teach journalism at a community college when I was too wrinkled and toothless to be on the air. This MA degree was my teaching ticket.

At that time, KING was owned by the Providence (Rhode Island) Journal Newspaper. ProJo, as we called it, actually helped pay tuition for employee education. (One of my fellow reporters used the benefit to go to law school!) I asked for and got Tuesdays and Thursdays off so I could attend classes during the day. On those mornings, I was able to walk our son Alex to school, which was a great time for mother-son bonding. My co-anchor on the weekends, David Kerley, also happened to be my neighbor. So we carpooled to the station most of the time. So yes, weekends worked for several years but I was ready for the next step.

The sale of the KING TV empire by the descendants of founder Dorothy Bullitt to the Providence Journal in 1992 marked the acceleration of corporate consolidation in the Seattle market. As the station moved from family to corporate ownership, there was a change in how promotions happened. This became even more obvious when ProJo sold the station in 1997 to the A.H. BELO corporation out of Dallas, Texas. Relationships and advancement resulting from years of personal effort, I thought, were diminished as the "old guard" was replaced by an influx of managers not necessarily steeped in the diversity or history of the Pacific Northwest.

For decades, Jean Enersen held the prized five, 6:30 and eleven weeknight newscasts. She could do that because she was KING's first female evening news anchor since 1972, the "Queen of KING." I filled-in for her when she took time off (which was significant considering her contract allowed her several weeks of vacation and all major holidays). Until 1998, KING had never had a weeknight news anchor of color — male or female. I told my news director, Eric Lerner, that I wanted a weeknight newscast "should the opportunity ever arise." I continued to work hard to "earn" the weeknight anchor position.

In late January of 1998, the station announced it had reached a multi-year contract with Jean which would basically get her off the eleven p.m. weeknight newscast. She would still anchor the five and 6:30 p.m. shows but not on

Fridays, which I would do. The station announced it would embark on a "nationwide search" for Jean's replacement at eleven. I had to audition with co-anchor Dennis Bounds (for chemistry!) even though I had been anchoring at KING for nearly fifteen years by then (Top Story, early mornings and weekends). Okay, I got it, no one gets a free ride. Fortunately, the viewing public called and wrote letters of support.

In May of 1998, a KING press release went out announcing I would be the eleven p.m. co-anchor with Dennis! Executive News Director Eric Lerner was quoted in an article by Kathy Hsieh in *Asian America at Large.*

"We had an excellent field of candidates. Lori's accomplishments as a journalist and ties to the community were a very important part of our decision."

In a letter, Glenn C. Wright, senior vice president of BELO's Television Station Group, wrote: "Based upon your excellent journalistic skills, history at KING, and presence in the community, I can think of no one better suited to assume this assignment for KING Television."

Some of my most treasured letters, however, came from friends in the community. *Seattle Times* CFO Mae Numata wrote: "You were the natural, and BEST choice! Thank you for continuing to be a terrific role model to others in the communications industry." And from B.J. Paine, an executive assistant and longtime KING employee, a note with a smiling avatar: "Congratulations! A "national" search could only bring to light that the best news anchor for eleven p.m. was right here!!"

I believe at the time of this decision, my news director was trying to address the elephant in the studio: the *whiteness* of Seattle weeknight anchor teams. In an interview with the *Seattle Times'* Kay McFadden a year later (July 4, 1999), I said, "I think there were concerns over hiring an Asian American woman;...It was like, weekends and mornings are fine, but do you want a woman of color as your prime-time standard bearer for the station? Things have progressed, but not completely."

Things began to accelerate. Eric Lerner left to become news director at WLS in Chicago. David Lougee became news director with a laser focus on making KING and its independent station, KONG, profitable. His solution was to create a ten p.m. newscast for viewers who wanted to get their news earlier than eleven. He couldn't do this on KING because a network affiliate station cannot step into NBC's "prime time" window of eight to eleven p.m. But he could sure do it on KONG, which is independent. Lougee believed viewers wanted a newscast at ten o'clock so they could go to bed earlier and get a jump on the morning commute, which was pretty horrendous. A locally produced newscast was also cheaper than syndicated programs like "Oprah" reruns, which were currently running at ten. In addition, the time slot was considered "wide open" since KSTW dropped its local newscast at ten in December 1998 after twenty-one years, leaving KCPQ, the local Fox affiliate, all alone at 10.

So starting on February 1, 1999, Dave assigned me to solo anchor "KING 5 News at ten on KONG." I told the *Northwest Asian Weekly* I was "very excited" by this added role which would accommodate viewers' lifestyles. What I didn't say was that the added newscast didn't come with added pay! After a shaky first newscast (we suffered three and a half minutes of black at 10:05) we ended the ratings period in positive territory. KONG had a two rating compared to KCPQ's seven rating. That's just about thirty thousand households watching KONG compared to a hundred thousand watching KCPQ. It was more than "Oprah" reruns were averaging (1.7 rating). Meanwhile, KING at eleven was number one in the market with a 9.8 rating (about 147,000 households) while KOMO was a close second at 9.2 (about 138,000 households).

Buoyed by the ratings, Lougee was eager to push for more "news on demand."

"Many viewers are missing our 6:30 p.m. newscast because they're stuck in traffic," he asserted. "We should provide a newscast at seven p.m. for them when they walk in the door." On September 2, 1999, the *Seattle Times'* Kay McFadden publicized that the new "KING 5 News at 7 on KONG" would begin October 4. And yep, I was going to anchor that newscast as well (again with no additional pay) with "a co-anchor to be named later." I took these developments as votes of confidence. KING managers were stepping up to recognize my ability as an anchor by putting me in a weeknight KING newscast at eleven as well as the seven and ten weeknight newscasts on KONG. Nothing prepared me for what was lurking around the corner.

On Friday September 24, 1999, just three weeks after McFadden's column, Lougee called me into his office. The conversation went something like this:

Lougee: Lori, I want to tell you before I announce this at the newsroom meeting. I've hired Margaret Larson to anchor the eleven p.m. news. She used to work for the network. (Margaret was a former NBC reporter who had moved to Seattle and was a former anchor at cross town rival KIRO/7.)

Lori: What?

Lougee: Oh, don't worry, you'll still anchor the seven and ten on KONG.

Lori: Why? (*Thinking to myself "Did I screw up or something?"*)

Lougee: We need you to build up viewership on the ten o'clock.

Lori: (*Speechless, thinking to myself, "The show on KONG that began just five months ago and has a two rating..."*

Lougee: Questions?

He started to get up to start the newsroom meeting.

Lori: When does this happen?

Lougee: I'm off next week, so the week after next.

I followed him out of the office and sat at my desk not daring to look around as he started gathering the newsroom staff.

"Big announcement," Lougee began. "I'm pleased to announce the hiring of Margaret Larson to anchor our eleven o'clock newscast on KING ..."

I don't remember what all he said. He was spinning it, saying how the station is relying on Lori and Allen Schauffler (Allen and I used to co-anchor the weekend news together) to build viewership on KONG at seven and ten.

I peeked up and gazed around the room. Most of my co-workers looked stunned. After Lougee left the newsroom, no one came by my desk. I couldn't blame them. What were they supposed to say? "Condolences?" "Sorry you lost the eleven?" "Bummer about getting kicked off KING and sent back to the minors?"

"I didn't know until ten minutes ago..." I said softly to Allen, who sat at the desk next to mine.

"Well, shit," he replied. He hadn't known about Margaret, either.

Almost instantly, my phone began to ring. Reporters from the *Seattle Times* and *Post-Intelligencer*! A sense of "Say nothing you'll regret" came over me and I tried to be honest and still go beyond "No comment."

Reporters: "Were you told why they took you off the eleven?"

Lori: "They said they wanted me to increase viewership on the ten o'clock. Wanted the eleven to *look different*."

Reporters: Was it because she's blonde and you're Asian?

Lori: "I don't know."

Reporters: "Are you considering legal action?"

Lori: "I still have some questions for Dave Lougee and (KING General Manager) Dennis Williamson."

The announcement percolated throughout the city all

weekend. Although I didn't know it, the station was getting bombarded with irate calls and mail from viewers protesting my removal from the eleven. The following Tuesday, September 28, John Levesque of the *P-I* came out with a column titled: "Matsukawa puts on brave face, but new job sure looks like a demotion." In it, he compared me to a Mariners baseball pitcher who is sent down to the minor league club after being in the home team's starting rotation.

"They're not cutting your pay. You'll actually get more mound appearances. But you'll no longer be in the big leagues, and the number of fans who will see you in Tacoma is a mere fraction of your audience when you were with the parent club," Levesque wrote. "Though admitting to disappointment at losing the eleven p.m. gig on KING, Matsukawa put on a brave face Friday. She said she was 'delighted' to be teaming with (Allen) Schauffler again and is embracing the challenge 'to kick some serious news butt at seven and ten' on KONG."

Levesque did not shy away from the poor optics KING showed by taking a person of color off one of its main weeknight newscasts. He quoted extensively from a letter to the station written by a Stanford classmate of mine and editor of the Asian American Theatre Revue, Roger Tang.

"It is particularly ironic that you take this action in a season where network programming has been accused of whitewashing the airwaves," Tang wrote. "Make no mistake about it. It *is* a demotion. Viewers are not stupid...It is *precisely* traditional thinking to move minority journalists off camera and shunt them to weekend slots and non-anchor slots. You may deny it to us, you may deny it to yourself, but the point is that it is your actions which speak loudest — and your actions speak volumes to this community."

In the same column LeVesque ended with: "... in a TV market where news anchors of color are scarcer than minorities in an NBC sitcom, Tang's accusation would make me squirm a little if I were a honcho at KING/5. Perception, after all, has a way of becoming reality." Yet in the very same column, Levesque said he didn't "believe for a minute" that the demotion was "racially motivated." He said while I was "a very good anchor," Margaret was better — "more authoritative, quick on her feet, more at ease on camera." Looking at this opinion in light of thirty-six years of anchoring at KING, I wonder how much of Levesque's idea of "better" anchoring was based on the fact that he was just not used to watching a woman of color anchor a newscast.

The reactions didn't end there. In an editorial titled "API Community Outraged over KING-TV's Decision to Move Lori Matsukawa" in the *International Examiner* dated October 1999, community activist Arlene Oki wrote, "When will television stations finally realize how important it is for communities of color to see people that look like us? It is, after all, a medium that depends on revenues from advertisers who sell products to people of color as well as people from the majority community." She also took issue with the *P-I*.

"And contrary to what John Levesque of the *Seattle Post-Intelligencer* thinks, Matsukawa is as quick with her responses, as comfortable in front of the camera, and connects well with the diverse viewership in the Seattle-King County region as well as anyone."

Viewers started sending letters to Dave Lougee and Dennis Williamson. Some sent copies to me. Kay Cooper of Everett, a viewer I didn't know, wrote to say that the last time she wrote a letter to KING was after the station let longtime meteorologist Jeff Renner go. (He was quickly hired back after a huge backlash from the public.) "And now, Lori Matsukawa! How could you? She seems like part of my family," Kay wrote.

Suzanne Hittman, whom I met while serving on the board of Asian Counseling and Referral Service, wrote: "Although I am Caucasian, I seek to live in a neighborhood and have community involvement which brings me in contact with persons of color. KING-TV news anchors ... will now all look like me, not like my neighbors and many of my friends. This is not the Seattle I know!"

I had no idea how KING's decision hurt and angered the Asian American community. In his column in the October 1999 issue of the Seattle Japanese American Citizens League newsletter, then-President David Yamaguchi wrote, "...Lori got a raw deal. While Lori's job-change is not strictly 'JACL news,' in a broad sense it touches everything we are striving for — fair treatment and fostering diverse talent in all fields." He encouraged people to express their displeasure to KING management.

I was blown away by supportive letters from three leaders in Seattle's Japanese American community: Tsuguo "Ike" Ikeda, past director of the Atlantic Street Center; Bob Sato, a member of the Nisei Veterans Committee, and Tosh Okamoto, one of the co-founders of Keiro Nursing Home (later, Nikkei Concerns).

Ikeda wrote: "Television ... plays a powerful role in communicating key values of respect, diversity and fair play so I strongly request changing management's decision on this demotion."

Sato: "We have greatly admired Lori's contribution to the many civic organizations in this region, and it is especially noteworthy that she projects that same spirit of service as she delivers KING/5 newscasts."

Okamoto: "I do not see the logic in replacing a loyal employee of many years with high ratings and following. Taking into consideration the large Asian market and being replaced by someone from the outside that seems to move frequently."

A few days after the announcement, Dave Lougee called me into his office. He was steaming.

"I'm not changing my mind," he said. "So call them off."

I was confused.

"What? Call who off?" I asked.

"All your friends you've told to write and call in," Lougee replied.

I had no idea about the public reaction that was pouring in. The station had long ago stopped distributing copies of the call-sheet to the newsroom.

"I haven't told anyone to write or call in," I said, flabbergasted.

Lougee did an eye roll. He didn't believe me.

"Oh come on, you're telling me you're not rallying people around you?"

"I'm not," I insisted. I was stunned, though a little part of me thought, "I never even thought of doing that! Maybe I should have."

Lougee hesitated. "You haven't?"

"No," I said. "If you're hearing stuff, it must be just happening on its own."

While it was true I didn't ask anyone to write or call the station, I did phone my union rep at AFTRA and an attorney friend to discuss a possible discrimination complaint. A Black anchor at another local station had tried that tactic, but ultimately she left the station and never worked in the Seattle market again. I quickly concluded it would be too difficult to prove racial discrimination, and I wanted to stay in Seattle to be a journalism voice for communities of color. Concern over whether I would file a discrimination complaint, however, may have been a reason I was called into General Manager Dennis Williamson's office a few months later. It was contract time and I imagined KING wanted to avoid a complaint from me and restore its tarnished public image. My representative (and a dear friend) Anthony "Tony" Hazapis and I negotiated a contract with better pay, more paid time off and holidays, and extended break times to attend Alex's school orchestra concerts. I also got the station to step up to the diversity plate and had them pay my AAJA Convention registration fee, travel and lodging costs.

A little over two years later, Margaret left KING to work for the relief organization Mercy Corps. I was asked to fill-in anchor on the eleven p.m. while the station conducted another nationwide search for her replacement. I occupied the eleven p.m. anchor chair until I retired seventeen years later.

CHAPTER 17
COMMUNITIES OF COLOR

If our son Alex ever felt he played second fiddle to the world, he never said so. I feel a pang of guilt when I think of the many community organization board meetings I dragged him to some weeknights. As we board members conversed around second-hand tables while drinking tea from Styrofoam cups, he busied his six-year-old self drawing volcanoes, kegs of dynamite and those Boris and Natasha bombs from "Bullwinkle" cartoons. He got really good at drawing Rube Goldberg-type mouse traps and setting up elaborate serpentine domino rallies. He was also the perfect reason to leave a meeting after an hour. It made for efficient meetings.

My KING TV co-anchor Mike James invited me to join my first community board. He was on the board of Asian Counseling and Referral Service, which provided behavioral health and social services to the area's underserved Asian American and Pacific Islander community. This was back in the Eighties when Dave Okimoto was the executive director, having just transitioned the agency out of its storefront office and into the Bush Hotel in Seattle's Chinatown-International District. It was the first time I was part of an organization that scheduled board meetings IN ADVANCE, had committees which were expected to deliver on commitments and required board members to help with fundraising. I was drawn to ACRS because it provided what so many AAPIs needed: services from people who spoke their language and knew their culture. The services ranged from a food bank that served culturally familiar food to citizenship classes, counseling for male domestic abusers to senior case management that came in the guise of lunch and exercise programs. The pan-Asian clientele, staff and board members reminded me of people in Hawai'i. Folks from all nationalities got along because no group was really the majority. Over the years, I appreciated watching the organization grow under executive directors Theresa Fujiwara and Diane Narasaki. They modeled dynamic and visionary female leadership. I learned other leadership qualities such as compassion and courage from fellow board members Emma Catague, Cris Baruso, Rocky Kim and Dolores Sibonga.

Once I dipped myself into the Chinatown-International District through ACRS, there was no turning back. I was adopted, some would say sucked, into Seattle's maturing minority activism scene, as a journalist observer. Seattle's communities of color began hitting their stride in the early Seventies. Asian Americans, African Americans, Latinos and Native Americans joined forces to notch political success in obtaining civil rights, jobs and social services. By the time I started working at Seattle TV stations, the men leading the communities were Larry Gossett, Jr., an African American; Bernie Whitebear, a Native American (Sinixt/Colville); Roberto Maestas, a Latino; and Bob Santos, a Filipino American. They became known as "The Gang of Four" or "The Four Amigos." The alliance was brilliant. They rallied their members to support each other's protests and demonstrations (hiring of Black contractors and workers, opposition to the Kingdome near the International District, occupation of Fort

Lawton and Beacon Hill School). The "Amigos" knew that gathering large numbers of demonstrators led to more media coverage and more bargaining power with authorities. Each time I needed to interview a member of an ethnic community for a story, the "Amigos" would oblige or, better yet, refer me to the best person on the topic. This was how I met DeCharlene Williams, Central District entrepreneur; Dawn Mason, state representative; The Reverend Samuel McKinney, head pastor at Mt. Zion Baptist Church; Tony Orange, civil rights pioneer; Ramona Bennett, Puyallup activist; Billy Frank, Jr., Nisqually fisheries activist; Tomio Moriguchi, retailer; Tsuguo "Ike" Ikeda, social services director; Lua Pritchard, AAPI cultural director; Francisco "Frankie" Irigon, social services director; Frank and Dorothy Cordova, historians; Bettie Luke, cultural leader; Cheryl Chow, city councilmember; Toru Sakahara, businessman; Seahawks head coach Tom Flores; and Estela Ortega, El Centro de la Raza director.

The fact that I was on television and seen hanging around the Chinatown-International District made me the "go to" emcee for all manner of community events. I sometimes felt like the "utility" Asian, as people asked me: "Are you Filipina? Are you Korean? Are you Chinese? Are you Japanese? Please emcee our event anyway."

Over the years, the invitations came from all manner of groups. I found myself emceeing events for education from preschool to college, Martin Luther King Jr. programs, women's programs, business programs and of course, journalism programs. So why do it? It was not for personal glory. Lord knows I could've used the time off. But I felt I was in a position to help shine a light on groups that needed attention, some TLC. So often, when I got that first, tentative call from a community member, the first thing I said after "Hello" was "What can I do for you?" There was such relief in their voice after that.

No matter how busy I got in "community business" there

was one person I could not refuse: Assunta Ng. Assunta was the publisher of the *Seattle Chinese Post* (later known as the *Northwest Asian Weekly*). It became a sort of joke around the political and fundraising world that nobody said "No" to Assunta. Not the mayor, not the King County executive, not any college president and certainly not any television or print reporter. We sort of felt sorry for Seattle's Gary Locke, who in 1997, became the first Chinese American governor in the United States. Assunta had given him a lot of press coverage when he was a state legislator and later, King County executive. Now as governor, he was hooked!

Assunta started her community newspaper in 1982, right after graduating from the University of Washington. She always reminded community members, particularly politicians, that "it's your job to be with the people. You work for them. You need them." As a member of our Asian American Journalists chapter, she pushed for inclusion of the community press. She gave annual community awards and for twenty years held a women's luncheon that honored women of color in various fields like medicine, sports and law. I asked her what drove her (and by default, her dedicated photographer husband, George Liu) to do so much for the community. She said simply, "If we don't make a big deal about what we do, nobody else will!" Of course, she was right.

The 1990s in Washington state saw many more people of color and their allies serving in important political offices. It made me proud to show this diversity in my reporting. For a time, Washington "just happened" to have a Black mayor of Seattle (Norm Rice), a Chinese American King County executive (Gary Locke) who was soon to be governor and a Black King County councilmember (Ron Sims) who would replace Locke as executive. On the Seattle City Council there were Dolores Sibonga, the state's first woman Filipino American lawyer; Cheryl Chow, Martha Choe and Richard McIver.

When I served on the board of the YMCA of Greater Seattle, the president was Richard A. Jones, now a United States District Court judge for the Western District of Washington. He was Quincy Jones' half-brother, although I never mentioned that to him the entire time I was on the board!

What I was seeing and reporting in Seattle about leaders of color was also happening across the nation. My personal role models were women of color.

Helen Zia, now an author and historian, gave up her job at the *Detroit Free Press* in the 1980s to become a media spokesperson for the Vincent Chin family. Chin died in a racially motivated beating in 1982 by two disgruntled auto workers who thought he was Japanese. Zia helped tell the Chin family's story, and her media savvy helped unite Asian Americans with new civil rights allies across the country to demand justice. She is smart, fearless and dedicated to the ideal of justice for all.

Irene Yasutake Hirano Inouye, founding president of the U.S.-Japan Council, believed in people-to-people connections to create positive relations between the United States and Japan. She sat at the conference table with presidents and prime ministers to establish student, professional and women's leadership programs. She was past chair of the Ford Foundation, past chair of the Kresge Foundation and founder and CEO of the Japanese American National Museum affiliated with the Smithsonian Institution. One of the little-known stories about Irene was how she helped leverage hundreds of millions of dollars from the Ford, Kresge and other foundations to lift Detroit out of bankruptcy in 2014. The rescue package prevented the Detroit Institute of Arts from selling its valuable collection of paintings and protected the pensions of Detroit city workers. Irene showed what mighty things can be accomplished so long as you're not concerned about who gets the credit.

In the beginning, covering community news was a

dilemma for me. I didn't want to be pigeon-holed as the "minority affairs" reporter, yet what good is knowledge of community issues and a robust network of spokespeople if I don't cover issues important to Asians, Blacks, Latinos and Indigenous folks? I couldn't assume my fellow journalists knew what was going on in the community. They didn't. Assunta Ng's words came back to me: "If we don't make a big deal about what we do, nobody else will!"

There was also a definitive line between covering a story and being the story. There were numerous times I had to step away from a story and pass it on to another reporter to avoid an appearance of conflict of interest. This is where Helen Zia's decision to quit her journalism job to serve as an advocate for the Vincent Chin family was instructive to me. Eventually, AAJA chapters began training community groups to become their own advocates to the media. I was proud to be a part of helping communities of color become their own storytellers.

CHAPTER 18
ALWAYS ON DUTY

The cartoon character "Inspector Gadget" had a tagline: "Inspector Gadget, always on duty." And when you sign up for this TV journalist gig, you pretty much become an Inspector Gadget. It meant responding to a news story whenever it crossed my path, getting a call early in the morning from a panicked producer asking for a contact number or giving you an urgent assignment. It sometimes interfered in family vacations or strained relationships with friends or relatives. Add to that the fear of being "scooped" and the deadlines of several daily newscasts being "always on duty" became all-consuming. It got even worse with the arrival of social media, where immediacy was what counted.

I COULD HEAR it almost before I felt it. A rumbling noise that got louder, as my kitchen floor vibrated wildly. On February 28, 2001, the Nisqually Quake rumbled for a minute at 10:54 a.m. through Western Washington. The epicenter was Nisqually, near the state capital of Olympia, magnitude 6.8.

"Earthquake!" I yelled and did exactly the wrong thing. I

stood in a door frame facing a wall of windows! My mouth hung open as I watched the chandelier in front of me sway left and right. By now, Larry had joined me in the door frame. The rumbling and shaking slowly ebbed.

"You okay?" Larry asked.

"Yep. You okay?" I replied.

"Yep."

"Okay, I'd better get to the station," I said as I hurried upstairs.

"I'll check for damage," Larry replied.

I drove straight to the station, not even contemplating that the highways might be damaged by what just happened. As soon as I got to KING, they put me into a newscar with a photographer. We were going to be the pool camera on the helicopter with the governor. As we lifted off, we could already see enormous cracks in the asphalt on several trails and roads in Olympia.

"Oh man, this is bad," said Governor Locke. "I hope no one was killed."

I tried not to get too dizzy staring at the ground below as the photographer asked the pilot to "circle one more time." We landed, did a quick interview with the governor and fed the video to all the stations right on the spot. *(There was one death, a heart attack, in the Nisqually Quake and about four hundred injuries. Damage was estimated at $1-4 billion.)*

On September 11, 2001, I was packing our son's lunch when he walked sleepily into the kitchen.

"Hey Mom," he mumbled. "A plane hit the Twin Towers." He had heard it on his clock radio. I hadn't bothered to turn on a TV or radio that morning.

"Oh, poor Twin Towers," I responded, naively thinking it must have been a small Cessna or something. I thought about how our family had just been up there a year earlier taking in the view.

I sent him off to school and climbed back into bed, eager

for a couple more hours of sleep. One day, I'll be off the night shift, I told myself. Less than thirty minutes later, Larry's alarmed voice woke me from a deep sleep.

"Hey Lori, you'd better get down here. You need to see this!" he hollered.

I ran downstairs and we watched in horror as New Yorkers ran through clouds of dust and the awful reruns showed jets exploding into the Twin Towers and the Pentagon.

"You've gotta get to the station," Larry began.

"Yep, I'm on my way," I replied. Sleep can wait. The phone rang. it was my mother.

"It's like the bombing of Pearl Harbor. This means war!" she cried into the phone. Mom and Dad were just ten years old during the attack on Pearl Harbor. Mom remembered seeing the Japanese Zeros flying over her house during the attacks.

I told her I was on my way to work, I'd call her later.

Once at the station, watching the video of all the bombed-out sites, my heart started beating fast. My friend from Hawai'i, Darryl Ching, was working at the Pentagon! Is he okay? I emailed and called; left messages, telling him to call me back. I wouldn't hear from him for several days. On September 23, he wrote a letter describing what he saw at the Pentagon. American Airlines Flight 77 crashed into the opposite part of the Pentagon from where he was working. He wrote that the area had just been renovated.

"The engineers had reinforced the structure with steel beams, shatter proof windows and Kevlar blankets. All of these renovations had undoubtedly saved lives," he wrote. "Unfortunately, we all knew some of the people who were killed." (*One hundred twenty-five Pentagon employees and contractors died plus fifty-nine passengers and crew aboard American Airlines Flight 77. An estimated 2,606 people perished in the Twin Towers.*)

Breaking news often happens when you least expect it, sometimes half a word away. In 2010, Larry and I were on a Mediterranean cruise with my parents when we were suddenly turned away from our destination, the port of Ashdod, Israel. Our ship's captain said the military was keeping commercial ships out of the port due to some sort of threat. We headed to Haifa instead. The "Gaza Flotilla Raid" erupted on May 31, 2010. Six civilian ships carrying humanitarian aid and construction materials were intent on breaking through an Israeli blockade of the Gaza Strip. Israeli soldiers boarded the Turkish *MV Mavi Marmara,* and shooting erupted. Nine activists were killed in the struggle including eight Turkish nationals and one Turkish American. The next day, during our land excursion to the River Jordan, we saw intense military activity, including low flying attack helicopters, trucks loaded with armed soldiers and trains hauling tanks and other gear toward Ashdod. When we returned from our land excursion, we were shocked to see the *MV Mavi Marmara* moored just yards away from us across the waterway! Authorities had towed it up to Haifa for further inspection. Mom and Dad had stayed on the cruise ship that day and reported seeing several warships, helicopters and even a submarine moving through the port. I talked to some fellow travelers (who turned out to be from Chehalis, Washington) and they said their relatives at home were worried about them. The reporting adrenaline kicked in. People in Washington state were worried about their relatives on a cruise ship in Israel! I picked up my stateroom phone and called the newsroom.

"Hi. It's me, Lori," I told the writer who answered. "Please transfer this call to the recording booth so I can give you a phoner (phone report)." I told viewers Washington residents onboard a cruise ship were rerouted to Haifa because of a flotilla raid near Ashdod. No one on the cruise ship was injured in the skirmish, but there was a heightened military presence in the air and on the streets of Israel. The Port of Haifa was filled with war vessels as the flotilla ship floated just yards from where I was standing. "At the Port of Haifa, Israel, Lori Matsukawa, KING 5 News," I concluded. Upon my return to Seattle, Executive Producer Norm Ohashi said, "Mats, I couldn't believe my ears! You were reporting from Israel!" I laughed, "Oops! Sorry, I thought I was working for CNN!"

It was a Thursday night. Dennis Bounds and I were in the middle of the eleven p.m. newscast when terrifying images began pouring in over the news feeds from Tohoku, Japan, where it was already March 11, 2011. Cars and huge ships were being carried away by black waves. Aerial video showed sea water swallowing up entire villages. I saw cars trying to outrun the deadly water, but I knew they wouldn't make it. I was still a novice with Facebook, but I began posting questions to Ross Mihara, a reporter friend who grew up in Aiea, my Hawai'i hometown. He was now an anchor for *NHK World* in Tokyo. "What's going on? Where is this happening? How high is the water?" I pressed "Post" and waited anxiously. Amazingly, he posted back almost immediately. "Water is several stories high. Fukushima Prefecture. Tokyo is pretty much at a standstill due to power outages. Trains stopped." I read some of the information on the air, as we still had a few minutes left in the newscast. As we left the air, Dennis and I agreed, this situation was really bad.

It so happened I took the next day off so my sister and I could fly to Las Vegas and surprise our mother on her birthday that Friday night. As we walked briskly toward our flight, I got a call from the news director.

"We might be sending you to Japan," Mark Ginther said. "You'll leave Sunday if we can get you a visa by tomorrow."

"I'm on my way to Las Vegas," I began.

"I'll call you when we know more," said Ginther and hung up.

My sister, Lisa, looked at me questioningly.

"Heck, we're going to surprise Mom tonight and that's that," I decided. "I can always fly back early tomorrow."

Lisa and I made our flight, checked into the hotel, lounged at the pool and got dressed for dinner. My cellphone rang. It was Larry.

"Ginther says he needs you to bring two passport size photos of yourself to the Japanese Consulate tomorrow," said Larry. Lisa pointed to her cellphone camera and nodded.

"We got it covered," I said.

We did indeed surprise Mom at dinner. She, Dad and my aunt were happy Lisa and I could join them for sushi and grilled fish under the stars. I apologized that I couldn't stay the entire weekend. Perhaps the only bright spot was that Lisa and I could cancel the rest of our room reservation penalty-free. At check out, I played the I-am-a-news-reporter-and-I-was-just-called-to-go-to-Japan card. It worked.

By Sunday, four of us (sports reporter and former Japan resident Andrea Nakata, field producer Greg Thies and videographer Doug Burgess) were on a plane to Narita Airport. I spent the flight thinking up stories we could pursue and made a mental note to call the Ishikawa family in Sendai. They were the family that hosted our son Alex when his Japanese class went to Japan in 2003. Tomoe Ishikawa attended Tohoku High School. She lived with her parents and grandparents in a farmhouse above the city.

Once through customs, I recorded my first report right there near the bus stop on the arrivals sidewalk. I showed viewers the granola bars I packed in my suitcase because at the time, flight attendants in Seattle warned us there might be food shortages in Tokyo. Riding the cab, I saw the city was just half-lit. Early the next morning, I checked out the Lawson store near the hotel. The bento cases were empty.

New technology allowed Greg to set up a studio and transmission spot right in his hotel room. He fed our video of the granola bars back to KING. I did a few live shots and "look lives" next to a window showing the empty streets and subway tracks behind me.

After seeing the television promotions of our crew in Japan, the daughter of University of Washington professors Gail Nomura and Stephen Sumida quickly contacted me by Facebook and said her parents were in Tokyo for a conference. I knew the Nomura-Sumidas from Blaine Memorial United Methodist Church in Seattle. Steve's family owns the Sumida watercress farm in Aiea, Hawai'i. We arranged to meet Nomura and Sumida outside a train station which was strangely quiet since many of the trains were idled by the earthquake. They told us on the day of the earthquake, their plane was diverted to a military base where they spent the night in a gym. Around us, young people were shouting for passers-by to donate for Fukushima relief. This was a Tokyo scene like I'd never seen before.

Greg Thies and I went back to Narita airport to cover the crowded but amazingly orderly scene there. Foreigners were heading home and some locals were taking unplanned vacations until utilities could be restored to their apartments. Study-abroad students had no choice but to leave when their schools shut down. We even found a few families heading to Seattle!

All this time, I was furiously trying to locate a driver to take our crew out to Fukushima Prefecture to see the tsunami damage. It was hard work because all the other news outlets (including all the networks) had already snatched the few who were willing to brave the broken roads and flooded countryside. Also, there was a fuel shortage, and it was expensive to fill a gas tank. The charges were astronomical.

I called Irene Hirano Inouye, president of the U.S.-Japan Council, because I knew she was in Tokyo, escorting a group of Japanese American leaders and introducing them to officials in Japan. She said she was trying to get their delegation home because of the chaos throughout the country. Among the delegates was the chair of JP Morgan Chase Pacific Northwest, Phyllis Campbell, a towering leader in the Northwest business world. I emailed Campbell and her assistant back in Seattle, gathered what travel information I could and sent it to KING, telling them to interview Campbell once she stepped off the plane at Sea-Tac airport. Campbell told us they were at a hotel conference table with select members of the Keidanren (Japan Business Federation) when suddenly the chandeliers started swaying and glassware on the table fell to the floor. While the Americans got up to leave, the Japanese "seemed somewhat unperturbed and continued with their dialogue," recalled Campbell. It took five minutes before everyone decided to leave the room. From the courtyard where they gathered, Campbell said they "were quite frightened" when they saw the tall buildings outside swaying visibly. No surprise, their next meeting with Prime Minister Naoto Kan was called off.

I did get through to Alex's exchange friend Tomoe Ishikawa in Sendai by phone. She said she was at work in an office in the city when the earth started shaking. Instinctively, she dove under her desk and thank God she did. The wall behind her crashed onto the desk, temporarily trapping her. She knew she had to get home to higher ground.

"And your parents? Your grandparents?" I asked.

"They are okay. The house got a few cracks, but no one got hurt," she assured me.

"*Odaiji ni* (take care)," I said, using one of the few Japanese phrases I knew.

As I hung up, I glanced at the television that was blasting CNN. I saw an image of a huge, ominous plume arising from the Fukushima Dai Ichi Nuclear Power Plant. Though I didn't know it then, our foray into disaster coverage was coming to an end.

Greg Thies rang my room.

"Pack your bags. They're bringing us home," he said.

"Wait. What? I'm *this close* to nailing a driver to take us to the tsunami area," I argued.

"All the airlines are moving their crews out of Tokyo to Osaka. The networks are getting out of Dodge," Greg replied.

"Tokyo is far from the plant! And the plume is heading out to sea, not south toward us. We can do this!" I pleaded.

"Our cab leaves tomorrow at nine. Make sure your bags are down there." He hung up.

We did one last standup in the hotel driveway about how we and other organizations were leaving Tokyo in light of the nuclear plant explosion. I still thought it was the worst time to be leaving. We got more video of the crowds at Narita. I gave away the rest of my granola bars to some American students in the lobby. On the flight back, I feared for Tomoe and her family and all the residents who were still assessing the death and destruction; all the residents fleeing the frightening, invisible radiation from the Fukushima Dai Ichi nuclear plant. I prayed for the people and vowed to come back to tell their story of recovery and resilience.

EVEN IN MY FREE TIME, I always felt I was still "on duty." Being on television means viewers feel they know you. They were always shouting out a greeting or, these days, asking for a selfie. I always obliged because it was great public relations for the station. I was grateful that people viewed me as a real person whom they could greet and have a conversation with.

My husband Larry got used to "the look" people gave when I passed them by on the street or in the grocery store. He became my PR wingman, stopping me mid-step and asking the shy student or TV fan if they wanted a photo with me. He then took the photo and sent them on their merry way. What a great guy.

Viewers in the Seattle area are really mellow, not like the screaming fans you see in Hollywood or on Broadway. They give "celebrities" their space and are surprised when I stop to answer their questions or better yet, ask THEM questions.

Some of the more interesting encounters happened when I least expected them:

- In a busy Manhattan subway stop on our way to a Mariners-Yankees playoff game, my photographer Dino DelaRosa and I heard, "Lori! Lori Matsukawa!" I looked up and there was one of my AAJA friends, Corky Lee! "You know people in New York?" marveled Dino. "Who woulda thunk?" I answered as the crowds swarmed around us.

- As Larry and I took a soft drink break near a small temple in Tokyo, we heard, "Lori Matsukawa, KING 5 News!" It was a community college official I had recently interviewed, also taking his soda break. Later, as we walked through another neighborhood, an excited group of young women surrounded Larry and me and begged for photographs. We didn't know who they were but apparently one of them may have been an exchange student in Seattle and word got out that "a famous television announcer" was in their midst. After much smiling and flashing of "peace" signs, Larry and I bowed our way furiously toward our hotel.

- Outside the Mariners' practice stadium in Peoria, AZ, a handful of my girlfriends and I were waiting at the exit gate, hoping to get some players' autographs. Some fans with us said, "Oh! Lori Matsukawa, can I have YOUR autograph?"

I laughed and said, "Sure."

Mona Locke, who was part of our girlfriends' group and probably the most famous of the bunch because she was still First Lady of Washington with her own bodyguard, jokingly raised her hands and shrugged, "What am I? Chopped liver?"

- The same group of girlfriends was walking to a mall in Shanghai when a bunch of young adults yelled across the lawn, "Lori Matsukawa! KING 5 News!" First of all, I don't know how they could have recognized me among a gaggle of Asian American women IN CHINA from such a distance.

We turned and I shouted back, "Hi! Where are you from?"

Instead of Seattle or Olympia, they yelled back, "Vancouver, B.C.!"

- When marijuana was legalized in Washington, I was curious about trying some of those edible products. What would the effect be? Would it even taste good? Larry and I were visiting one of his relatives in Omak. While cruising along the rural road back to town, we spotted side-by-side pot shops.

"Let's buy some chocolates here," I chirped. "It's so remote, in the middle of nowhere! No one will see us!"

Larry and I went into a shop and bought a few chocolates, hard candies and marijuana tea. As we headed to our car, a voice yelled out, "Lori? Lori Matsukawa? Fancy meeting you here!"

I froze in my tracks and looked across the lot. Larry grabbed the brown paper bag out of my hand and swung around to the driver's side of our car.

It was a man I'd never seen before. He walked up smiling

and shook my hand. He was the editor of a marijuana industry magazine.

"Out here doing some research? Planning to do a story on this for KING 5, I bet," he said. I forced a smile and thought, "Brilliant!"

"Yes," I said. "I'm pretty interested in doing a story about growers in our state, especially those who are doing it hydroponically instead of in the ground or containers."

So much for being in the middle of nowhere.

- For our twenty-fifth wedding anniversary, Larry and I took a week-long trip to Amsterdam/Paris. On the last night before our flight home from Amsterdam, we had a lovely dinner at a small cafe.

"Well," said Larry, "We've been in Paris for a week, and no one has recognized you. How about that?"

Suddenly, a young man at the table right next to ours said, "Oh, you're Lori Matsukawa. You work at KING 5."

"Yes," I stammered, almost laughing out loud at Larry's surprised face. The man continued.

"I'm Patrick Tisdale. You interviewed my mom, Betty, for a news story."

"Yes, of course, I remember Betty," I replied. "She was a nurse in Vietnam who cared for orphans."

Larry and I still laugh about this encounter to this day!

CHAPTER 19
A DEFINITIVE
PIECE OF WORK

As retirement loomed, I began to think about my journalistic legacy. I found it true that journalism — according to Alan Barth in the *New Republic* back in 1943 — was "the first rough draft of history."

All those first-person interviews that were hurriedly conducted, edited and aired only to be stuffed under my desk were historic accounts. People in the future will want to know how and why certain things happened. And of course, there are as many histories as there are people to recall them. I looked at the cardboard boxes under my desk stuffed full of newspaper clippings, videotaped interviews and spiral Reporter's Notebooks that I had collected over the years. A lot of them held the story of Japanese American wartime incarceration and the campaign for redress. They were events that took place here in the Northwest from the 1940s through the 1980s.

"When I die," I thought, "what will KING TV have in its archive that contains — in one place — the entire arc of the incarceration story as recalled by the people here who experienced it?" I decided then and there that I would create a definitive piece of work, a resource, a simple-to-find, archival "File Tape" for future KING TV journalists.

I began researching in earnest in 2015, even attending a Minidoka Pilgrimage that summer to visit the old concentration camp site which is now a National Park Service Interpretive Center near Hunt, Idaho. The bus ride was more than eight hours long. I met many potential subjects to include in my report: people who were incarcerated there as children; local farmers who remembered the presence of the neighboring camp; researchers and professors who wanted to know more about daily life in camp and the social harm caused by the unjustified incarceration of an entire people without due process. I was so intent on airing the special on the seventy-fifth anniversary of Executive Order 9066 in February 2017, I passed up a voluntary retirement offer from KING. The offer required senior staff to retire by April 2016. Among those who took the offer were longtime anchor Jean Enersen, who had been there forty-eight years, and meteorologist Jeff Renner, who was first hired at KING in 1977. Dennis Bounds and I were both offered a retirement package, but only one of us could take it. Since I had seniority, I had the right to accept or decline first.

"I can't retire now!" I exclaimed to Larry at home. "I'm in the middle of writing my opus, my big deal story on the camps for the seventy-fifth anniversary!"

"How important is the story for you?" Larry asked.

I thought about it for a moment.

"Really important," I concluded. "If I don't do it, who's going to do it? I have all this crap I've saved, for what, if I just walk away?"

When I told Dennis he could take the package, he was flabbergasted. "Are you sure?" he kept asking.

"Yes," I assured him, and I meant it from my heart. "I've got too much stuff to finish that airs in February 2017. I need to stay."

Of course, this was a pretty brazen assumption on my part since my news director Cheryl Carson had not signed off on airing my series or doing a documentary in February 2017. I made my pitch to her in June and my "Governor in China" videographer Dave Wike and I left for the Minidoka Pilgrimage in July.

"This series will air over five days and cover the entire arc of the incarceration story," I said, drawing a rainbow in the air with my hands. "We'll start with the camps, but what happened after they left the camps? That's part two. Then there's the little-talked-about resentment between families whose sons went to war and those whose sons went to jail for resisting. Then there was the campaign for redress which was organized largely by folks here in the Northwest."

Cheryl was surprised to learn that a freshman Irish American from Seattle named Mike Lowry sponsored the first redress bill in Congress in November 1979. In the book *Born in Seattle: The Campaign for Japanese American Redress*, Lowry's aide Ruthanne Kurose explained how Lowry introduced the bill as a "civil liberties" issue rather than a "Japanese American only" issue to broaden its appeal to other members of Congress. Whatever happened, Lowry insisted that monetary payment be included in the final legislation for those who were forced into camp

I wrapped up the pitch with a flourish.

"And finally, how is the incarceration story retold today? Why, through the arts!" I could finally showcase the many works of art I had preserved on video over the years expressing the outrage and despair of the experience. A painting by art professor Roger Shimomura, a modern Japanese *butoh* dance for children, an immersive opera at Seattle Opera and the *piece de resistance*, a spoken word performance by Troy Osaki, a local law student.

"Are you talking to anyone who lived in the camp?" Cheryl asked.

Dave and I were almost giddy. "Yes! We are going to Minidoka with a woman who lived there as a young girl." I didn't say that Fumiko Groves had cancer and that this would probably be the last time she would visit.

"Our coverage of the pilgrimage will easily fill an hour-long documentary," I promised. Dave said the desolate Idaho farmland would make awesome photos.

Cheryl ordered up supporting materials for viewers including a graphic video describing how incarcerees were allowed to bring only what they could carry and a dedicated website with lists of other incarceration-themed happenings around town.

She was sold.

After our meeting, I sat at my desk and looked at the boxes of old notes. Cheryl was ONE person who was beginning to understand the gravity of what wartime incarceration meant to an entire generation of people. It took seventy-five years to get this far. The urgency of my project was real.

To understand why the incarceration story lives large in the Pacific Northwest requires knowledge of what families of Japanese descent went through during World War II. Having been raised in Hawai'i, I had to learn about the experience through my Northwest "aunties and uncles."

I first heard about the Japanese American Citizens League (JACL) in Portland in 1979 when I was invited to dinner at the home of Dr. Homer and Mikki Yasui. Homer had seen "the new Japanese anchorlady" on television and gave me a cold call. I guess he was the unofficial "greeter of Japanese folks" in town. It turned out his brother was Minoru Yasui, an attorney who challenged the constitutionality of wartime curfews during World War II. (Four landmark cases regarding incarceration went to the U.S. Supreme Court during the war: *Yasui v. United States,*

Hirabayashi v. United States, Korematsu v. United States and *Ex parte Endo*.)

I didn't actually join the JACL until I came to Seattle to work at KOMO in 1980. A bearded gentleman named Sam Shoji literally stopped me on the street in the Chinatown-International District and invited me to a meeting. Sam, like Homer, was Seattle's version of the unofficial "greeter of Japanese folks."

"You're the new reporter at KOMO," Sam said, looking up at me, his beard fluttering in the wind. "You should come to our JACL meeting."

I eventually joined the chapter's Scholarship Committee and was asked to deliver some flyers to Sumi Yoshioka, the organist at Blaine Memorial United Methodist Church. She reminded me of so many of my aunties back in Hawai'i.

"You should come check out our service," she invited.

Blaine — a historically Japanese American congregation — became my "home church." Larry and I were married there in 1982, and we spent more than ten years producing the church Christmas pageants. Larry did the writing and directing; I played the piano or hit the tape recorder. Many youngsters, now grown, still laugh about the "trauma" we inflicted upon them "forcing" them to wear Christmas trees on their heads, dance like King Herod's harem girls or sing Christmas songs in Spanish and Japanese.

Several "community activists" counted themselves among Blaine's congregation, such as Dave Okimoto (executive director at Asian Counseling and Referral Service), Tsuguo "Ike" Ikeda (executive director at Atlantic Street Center), Chuck Kato (a longtime supporter of a Japanese cultural center) and Joey and Vera Ing who were Chinese American but Vera, an urban planner and community activist, grew up in the same Chinatown-Central District neighborhood as many Japanese Americans. Red-lining by banks back in the day pretty much restricted Asian families to Beacon Hill, the

Chinatown-International District and the Central District. Joey was an architect from Hawai'i and together the Ings were a power couple in Seattle's social and political scene. Toshikazu (Tosh) Okamoto worked for the Seattle Fire Department and was the first ethnic minority hired as a mechanic. He volunteered countless hours to document the heroism of Nisei veterans and helped found a senior citizens nursing home for Nikkei.

On many Sundays, I'd be button-holed by one of the "movers" to have KING TV cover a certain community gathering, demonstration or City Council meeting for a variety of reasons, but mostly to highlight what was happening in the community. Over the years, "community" became shorthand for "communities of color" or — depending on the speaker — the Japanese American or Asian American community. In the early Eighties, the requests focused increasingly on the redress movement, which began in 1970. The organizers were seeking redress from the federal government for the incarceration of 120,000 people of Japanese ancestry in government concentration camps during World War II. And, no surprise, many of the initial organizers were members of the Seattle Chapter of the Japanese American Citizens League. In my opinion, Seattle became the birthplace of the redress movement because an estimated 12,892 (Historylink.org, David Takami) people of Japanese ancestry in our state were deprived of their property and businesses and incarcerated in 1942 for no cause and without due process. More than nine thousand of them came from Seattle alone. The first Japanese community in the nation to be herded onto trains was from Bainbridge Island.

Many Seattle families ended up in Minidoka, considered a "regular sized" camp holding just over 9,300 inhabitants. It was located near the farming community of Hunt, Idaho. A thousand young men from Minidoka volunteered for the U.S. Army's renowned all-Japanese 442nd Regimental Combat

Team (RCT), 100th Battalion and Military Intelligence Service, the most of any camp.

And two of the four Supreme Court challenges to the curfew and incarceration laws came out of the Northwest: *Yasui v. United States* and *Hirabayashi v. United States*.

Being familiar with the JACL allowed me to meet and interview some of the organizers of what would become a national movement: Cherry Kinoshita, Chuck Kato, Henry Miyatake, Ken Nakano, Shosuke Sasaki and Ron Mamiya. It also allowed me to get in on the "ground floor" and document the progress of the movement as a news story that would become part of Pacific Northwest and U.S. history. There were many stories to tell, since the incarceration and its effect on the Japanese American community was so complex. Simply reporting what happened was challenging because many of those in the Issei and Nisei (first and second) generations didn't want to talk about the unconstitutional and humiliating events they experienced forty years before.

During commission hearings held across the country in 1980-81, some of the speakers broke down in tears revealing for the first time their feelings of violation and betrayal. One of the speakers at the Seattle hearing was Sam Shoji, his long white beard quivering with emotion. What an amazing day it was for me to cover the presentation of Seattle's first redress check of twenty thousand dollars to an elderly Issei man in 1990. There was great urgency to put checks into the Isseis' hands, since they were dwindling by the day forty-five years after the end of the war.

Another aspect of the incarceration story I covered was the legal effort to overturn the U.S. Supreme Court cases when new evidence was discovered. A researcher discovered documents that showed federal attorneys had suppressed evidence that would have proved the Japanese communities were not a security threat. JACL contacts made it possible for me to interview Gordon Hirabayashi and his team of "young

Turks" who would argue his *coram nobis* case before a federal judge in Seattle. I was also thrilled to interview Gordon's original attorney when Gordon was still a University of Washington student challenging the curfew law. During our interview, Arthur Barnett, surrounded by piles of manila folders on his desk, pointed and gestured, all fired up over the lack of due process suffered by Japanese Americans. Much to Barnett's satisfaction, in 1987 a federal judge in Seattle agreed with Hirabayashi's team and ruled the U.S. Supreme Court made an error in his case and might have come to a different conclusion had it been given complete evidence.

And then there were the veterans and their less-discussed brethren, the resisters. The Nisei Veterans Committee was more than a social club for Japanese American vets and those who served in the Military Intelligence Service. The men who played basketball in the gym and cooked up sukiyaki dinners in the large kitchen were living, breathing history. They told and retold the stories of their service. Many volunteered from the incarceration camps where their families were being held. Some fought in the most brutal campaigns of World War II.

In October 1944, the 442nd RCT and 100th Battalion were sent in to rescue "The Lost Battalion" — Texans in the 36th Division trapped behind enemy lines in France's Vosges forests. While 211 Texans were rescued, some eight hundred Nisei soldiers were killed or injured.

"The trees were so thick, and it was so foggy, you couldn't see ten feet ahead," Ted Oye told me. "Then PEWW! A shot blew my helmet off!" He said a friend later found his helmet with a bullet hole in it. When the friend saw Ted, he shouted, "Ted! I thought you were dead!"

"No," Oye laughed. "I'm not dead. I'm still here."

The Battle of the Lost Battalion would prove to be costly.

"The guys said, 'That's suicide!'" recalled Roy Fujiwara when the men first heard the order. "That's suicide!"

Fujiwara shook his head and looked me straight in the eye. "But you know what they say, 'Go for Broke.'"

The unit paid a heavy price. K Company had been reduced from about 180 men to seventeen. I Company, of similar size, had only four riflemen and a few machine gunners. Before a hastily planned ceremony to present the Presidential Unit Citation, General John E. Dahlquist scolded the Unit's Lt. Colonel Virgil Miller.

"Colonel, I told you to have the whole regiment out here!" witnesses heard the general snarl.

Roy shook his head at the memory. "The colonel said, 'Sir, this *is* the regiment. This is all I have left. This is all I have left.'"

In April 1945, the 442nd and 100th were sent to Italy to join the 92nd Division and try to break through a heavily fortified mountain ridge called the Gothic Line. For five months, the German army had stymied the Allies. It was decided the 442nd would serve as a decoy, by going up three thousand feet of steep, craggy mountainside in the dark … in silence … to surprise the enemy. Three soldiers did fall to their deaths. But neither they, nor any of their fellow soldiers, made a sound.

In two days of fierce fighting, the Nisei soldiers were able to accomplish what no other Allied unit had done: break through the Gothic Line and force the Germans to retreat. But the victory came at a high price. Thirty-two Nisei died and dozens were injured.

Meanwhile, in the jungles of China-Burma-India, six thousand Nisei soldiers served in the Military Intelligence Service. The MIS soldiers were responsible for gathering intelligence from the Japanese army, interrogating POWs and breaking secret codes. The existence of Japanese American intelligence soldiers in the Asian theater was so secret, they were forbidden to talk about their service until their exploits were declassified in 1972 through Executive Order. In the renowned guerilla group known as Merrill's Marauders (named after their leader Brigadier General Frank Merrill) white soldiers of the 5307th Composite Unit were specifically told to protect the fourteen MIS members, as they were considered the "eyes and ears" of the unit. Merrill himself wrote: "As for the Nisei group, I couldn't have gotten along without them."

"The intelligence work of the MIS is credited with shortening the war and saving lives," Hiro Nishimura told me in December 2004. It was at the last luncheon gathering of the MIS Northwest Association. They were disbanding because their members were aging and dying.

"You know about Roy Matsumoto?" Hiro asked. I shook my head.

"Ranger Roy is what we call him," said Hiro. (Matsumoto was living in Gig Harbor at the time but would eventually move to San Juan Island.)

"He was with Merrill's Marauders in Burma. They were surrounded behind enemy lines and Roy shouted: *Susume!* 'Charge!' in Japanese. The Japanese soldiers thought it was an order from their commander and they jumped up. The Americans just mowed them down."

Again, the incarceration story is complicated. Yes, the incarceration was unjust. Yes, the exploits, service and sacrifice of the Nisei soldiers and MIS were mind-blowing. But there was also the divisive issue of the resisters. I interviewed two such men who, according to Frank Abe, a former reporter and now author, were ostracized by the Nisei vets and their families for much of their postwar lives.

"Jim Akutsu paid for his honesty for the rest of his life," mused Abe.

Jim Akutsu was a "No-No Boy." He had answered "No" to questions twenty-seven and twenty-eight on what was referred to in the camps as the "loyalty questionnaire."

"It asked me if I would forswear loyalty to the emperor

and pledge allegiance to the United States," Akutsu told me. "Well, I never was loyal to the emperor, so I had nothing to forswear." By answering "no and "no," Akutsu was labeled "disloyal" by the army. He and dozens of others were separated from their families and put into the Tule Lake Relocation Camp in California. They were snubbed by men who volunteered for the army, who thought they were too "chicken" to prove their loyalty by picking up a rifle.

"Those No-No Boys," one veteran told me with a look of disgust, "They would not swear loyalty to the United States."

Frank Yamasaki resisted the draft from Minidoka where his family was incarcerated. He believed he and all the others of Japanese ancestry were unjustly locked up. For that, he served time at McNeil Island Penitentiary. Some forty years later in our interview, the memories still brought him to tears.

"They said I had to [join the army to] prove I was a loyal American. Well, I AM a loyal American!" he wept. I was stunned and looked down at my lap. I had never seen a Nisei man cry before. But I kept sitting with him and my photographer kept on rolling.

I made sure I was in Washington D.C. in November 2011 when the Nisei Vets were recognized with the Congressional Gold Medal. As House Speaker John Boehner welcomed the roomful of white-haired men, many in wheelchairs, I saw their beaming faces. How proud they were that they had served their country so well!

One vet said quietly, "No one can ever question our loyalty again."

(*Author's Note: The incarceration series and half-hour special "Prisoners in Their Own Land" aired February 14 to 19, 2017, marking the seventy-fifth anniversary week of the signing of Executive Order 9066. It took videographer Dave Wike and me more than a year to research, film, write and edit the series, which also included its own website landing page and graphic animation. The stories were heavily promoted by the station. When the first piece aired on Monday February 14, 2017, President Donald Trump had just issued an executive order banning travelers arriving from predominantly Muslim countries. The newsroom received several irate calls from viewers who thought we were purposely comparing President Trump's executive order to that of Franklin Roosevelt's EO 9066 in 1942, which put 120,000 people of Japanese ancestry in American concentration camps. We explained to them it was merely a coincidence that "Prisoners in Their Own Land" was airing on the same day as the president's action. The story, we explained, had been months in the making. Later, several of us in the newsroom sat back and discussed the power a president could wield through an executive order. In the months to come, Japanese American groups rallied in support of Muslim communities, claiming Japanese Americans had the "moral authority" and responsibility to reject race- or religion-based executive orders. The series won a regional Emmy award, my first, in 2018.)*

In 2015, I came across a press release from the White House announcing THREE people from the Pacific Northwest were getting the Presidential Medal of Freedom, America's highest civilian honor. I jumped out of my chair! On the list were the resister Minoru Yasui (posthumously); Native American fishing rights advocate Billy Frank, Jr. (posthumously) and William Ruckelshaus, who served as the first administrator of the Environmental Protection Agency but was better known as the U.S. deputy attorney general who resigned rather than fire special prosecutor Archibald Cox as ordered by President Richard Nixon. The event is widely known as the "Saturday Night Massacre" and took place during the Watergate scandal.

"I've gotta cover this!" I declared and looked worriedly at the date of the event. It was happening in less than a week!

Thankfully, Assignment Manager Cynthia Wise knew how to get me White House credentials, and I was on my way. By that year, we KING reporters were encouraged to record and send video from our smartphones. The day I arrived, I videotaped promos in front of the White House giving viewers a preview of the ceremony that would honor the three Northwesterners. I had to hurry as the sun was setting and I had to send the promos to the newsroom immediately for that evening's newscasts. The "one take" promo is the result of years of having to promote a story quickly with no time to edit it. It has to be done on the first try, smoothly and accurately, because it would be aired or posted on the station's website immediately.

The next day in the East Room, as I crouched among the tripod legs on the press platform, I was delighted to see a famous face — James Taylor — on stage. He was getting a medal that day, too! As I watched President Obama present the medals, I quickly flashed back to the time I dreamed of being a network correspondent. Here I was, in the White House, covering the president in action. What if I had chosen to work for the network? Could I have done the job? This day, I felt the answer was "Yes." That night, doing my live shot from a press tent outside the White House, I WAS a network correspondent, albeit one for the KING network.

CHAPTER 20
THE JAPANESE CULTURAL & COMMUNITY CENTER OF WASHINGTON

don't know why I agreed to help create a Japanese cultural center in Seattle. Was it an idea that had been rattling in the back of my head? Was I captivated by the idea of starting something significant to celebrate my culture and the role the Japanese played in Seattle's history? Maybe it was just that I was asked by two community-minded supporters I respected.

Kip Tokuda, a department head for Family and Children's Services in Seattle, was a recently retired (2002) Washington state legislator His father, George, grew up in Japanese Gulch where workers at the Mukilteo Lumber Company lived. While he was in the Minidoka concentration camp, George, a pharmacist, lost his two drug stores. In a letter from Minidoka dated March 24, 1943, to his friend Clara Pokswinski Kane he wrote: "I have lost everything totally … worth at least ten thousand dollars … the fruit of my seven years of hard work and sacrifice."

After the war, George reopened a drug store in Seattle's Nihonmachi. It was among a few businesses listed in the Seattle version of "The Green Book" that welcomed and served African American travelers. Kip's mom, Tama, became a writer and actress in local theater in her later years. Kip served in the Washington state legislature from 1994 to 2002. His sister Wendy was the news anchor who let me shadow her when I was an intern at KPIX. Kip was a known community booster. He also had the worst Japanese accent, which always amused me. It was like running into those Stanford students at the campus tea house who mispronounced their own Japanese names!

Ron Mamiya was a Seattle municipal court judge who volunteered scores of hours campaigning for redress in the late Seventies through mid-Eighties. Ron's parents, like Kip's, were Nisei. They owned the Sagamiya Confectionery store on Main Street in Nihonmachi. During meeting breaks, Ron often reminisced about the delicious baked *manju* and soft mochi cakes that flew off store shelves. In 2003, Ron went to Japan for the first time as part of a group called the Japanese American Leadership Delegation or JALD. It was an epiphany. He told me he was instantly transformed. He wanted to reclaim his Japanese history and culture that had been repressed in the postwar years.

The three of us made a good team. Ron did much of the legal work to transition ownership of the century-old Japanese Language School buildings from the Nisei volunteers to the Sansei and younger volunteers. Kip lobbied the legislature and the governor's office for a million dollars in funding to refresh the buildings. That brought in new clientele to lease office space, study Japanese language and enjoy cultural activities such as festivals, historic exhibits, judo, karate and taiko classes. The seniors loved gathering in the Japanese language library for tea and conversation, and we opened a gift shop, filled with donated Japanese treasures from the community. I became the "face" of the center, responsible for raising matching funds within the community.

In the end, I visited sixteen families who agreed to become founding families, raising eight hundred thousand dollars for the now renamed Japanese Cultural and Community Center of Washington (JCCCW).

None of this amazing transformation would have happened, though, without a chance meeting between me and an ample, bearded, bespectacled Caucasian man named Bif Brigman. Bif was proof that "being Japanese" was as much mental and spiritual as it was physical. Ron, Kip and I were looking for someone to run the fledgling cultural center in 2004. Someone mentioned a guy named Bif who was running an art gallery in the Roosevelt neighborhood. I walked into his pleasantly cluttered shop and introduced myself. During our conversation, Bif told me how he admired Japanese American and Japanese artists, especially painters and sculptors. I learned he knew a lot about applying for grants and finding money to support the arts and culture. Later, I realized he had a photographic memory and could retrieve even the most obscure document or email because he remembered where everything was!

Bif agreed to come to the JCCCW as programming director because he truly believed the executive director should be Japanese.

"It just looks better," he told me.

As it turned out, this tall, bear-like gentleman would be just the bridge we needed between the Japanese nationals who ran the language school, the Nisei who ran the finances and the Sansei who were trying to grow the center for future generations. On occasion, I dropped by the center and there was Bif, strolling down the well-worn hallway wearing a *hapi* coat one of the Japanese language school teachers had made for him. There was a lot of laughter and joking. Sometimes I found him discussing the distinction between Kutani and Imari porcelain with a collector who stopped by the center's gift shop. And often, we employed him as a "go between" with the Nisei to help mediate a maintenance problem or community dispute.

Yet the most amazing thing about Bif was his ability to get things done using *other people's money!* His ability to rally volunteers to fund and complete the $1.8 million update of the cultural center buildings was jaw-dropping. He was a project manager extraordinaire who could write grant requests, get them funded and track them until the project was done. Even smaller projects — like doing genealogy research and publishing it in the community newspaper — were funded through shrewd negotiations and grants. Bif convinced local architect Jerry Arai to display an enormous triptych by University of Kansas professor and Seattle born artist Roger Shimomura that Jerry and other art patrons had purchased. Jerry and his friends had bought the art with the intent of displaying it in a brand new building. It was put in storage. Bif said it was a shame to have such a piece tucked away. He found a way to properly display and protect the masterpiece. Today, "Nikkei Story," depicting three generations of Japanese in America, adorns the center's main conference room. Bif even convinced the very exacting Ina Tateuchi, a local philanthropist, to pay for the restoration of an original silk calligraphy presented in 1901 by Hirobumi Ito, Japan's first prime minister, during a visit to Seattle. It cost thousands to have a craftsman in California repair it.

Through his many years with the JCCCW, Bif treasured the century-old buildings, built by the determined Issei immigrants. He fought hard to keep its historic designation, and that's where conflict emerged. Some board members thought it would be best to tear down the old buildings and start anew. We debated whether to pursue delisting the campus from historic status. Thankfully, we didn't. Bif eventually moved on to other community projects such as the Minidoka

Pilgrimage and the *International Examiner's* Advocacy Journalism Fellowship Program. But his strong vision of a historic place where people could gather and celebrate Japanese and Japanese American culture was a gift he gave to me.

As with any generational transition, there were a few bumps. The Nisei folks and their peers who arrived from Japan as war brides or company workers were loath to give up control of the buildings to the "young guys." (Keep in mind, we weren't young! In 2003, Kip was fifty-six, Ron was fifty-four and I was forty-seven.) They just thought we didn't know what we were doing.

During one of our cultural center summer rummage sales, I paused from sorting items in the alley and simply leaned against Building One. I was feeling defeated. The negotiations over the transition had been going on for months and the Nisei weren't budging. Tsuchino Forrester, who along with her husband Mike were founding family members, was close by.

"Tsuchino," I finally sighed. "Why are we fighting so much?"

Tsuchino had come to America from Japan years ago after marrying Mike, who served in the military. She was now the business manager for Mike's computer business. She looked at me with her large eyes and shook her head slowly.

"I don't know," she replied. "You know, we all want the same thing. To keep this place in the community."

"Yes," I said. "We want to keep this center alive, we really do!"

The negotiations went quickly after that heart to heart. The final agreement was carefully negotiated with Bill Tashima of the Seattle JACL serving as a mediator. It allowed the Nisei to regain control of the building if the finances started to go south. It was up to the "young guys" to prove we could be trusted.

Over the years, the JCCCW shone through as the only

place in the region where people from Japan and Washington state could gather, celebrate Japanese culture and leave saying, "I have a friend in America!" or "I have a friend in Japan!" During the 2011 Tohoku earthquake and tsunami disaster in Japan, calls poured in from all over Seattle from people wanting to know how they could help the victims. I was so grateful we had staff and volunteers on hand who could speak both English and Japanese to guide callers to the American Red Cross and translate messages for them to send to their friends in Japan. Our staff and volunteers joined Governor Chris Gregoire outside a Sounders soccer game to collect donations for disaster victims.

The center's profile grew again when it partnered with the University of Washington's Department of Landscape and Architecture in 2014 to construct its Kintsugi Garden. *Kintsugi* is the Japanese art of fixing broken pottery using melted gold. In the garden, the irregularly cut pavers are "held together" with bronze, representing how the Japanese American community was broken when families were sent to wartime concentration camps. But now, the community is back, healing and is perhaps even more beautiful in its brokenness and repair.

The center is also a "must see" for all new Japanese consuls general who rotate into Seattle every two or so years. The Consulate staff confided it provides a one-stop history lesson for the diplomats, who value the contributions of the Japanese pioneers. They are sometimes shocked to hear about the wartime incarceration camps and how families returning from them lived in the center's classrooms because no one would rent them a place. Of course, they are pleased that Japanese language and martial arts are among the many activities still enjoyed at the center.

As time went on, the center's programming got better, school enrollment grew and the building refurbishing lifted everyone's spirits. Eventually, the Nisei stepped back. The cynical among us would say they just got old and tired. But make no mistake, they remain watchful. We "young guys" learned that to build trust, we needed to continually express obligation, *on*, and appreciation, *okage sama de*, for all that the Nisei and Japanese nationals had done. Which, when you think of it, was a lot.

CHAPTER 21
U.S.-JAPAN DIPLOMACY — AN "AHA!" MOMENT

learned a lot about diplomacy from a professional diplomat. It was 2016 in Seattle. I was interviewing Ichiro Fujisaki, the former Japanese ambassador to the United States.

"Mr. Ambassador, who do you think will win the race for U.S. President, Hillary Clinton or Donald Trump?" I asked.

The ambassador, looking suave in his dark suit and carefully combed hair, took a deep breath and smiled.

"Elections are like a Christmas present," he said with his slight British accent and a twinkle in his eye. "You open it and exclaim, 'This is just what I wanted!'"

How I came to be in his orbit could be traced to a visit to Japan back in 2005.

I was selected by the Seattle consul general that year to represent Seattle in the Japanese American Leadership Delegation (JALD). You recall my fellow JCCCW co-president Ron Mamiya had gone on the first delegation in 2003. It turned him into a blazing Japanophile. He told Kip Tokuda, our other co-president, to go in 2004. Kip returned equally stoked, re-doubling his efforts to fund improvements at the center. They both encouraged me to apply for the program. I was selected to be on the JALD team in spring of 2005. The idea of JALD was to bring a group of young Japanese American leaders from across the country to Japan to meet lawmakers, corporate executives and educators. The person leading our group was the intrepid Irene Hirano, my longtime role model. Irene truly believed in people-to-people relationships. These ties, she said, could lead Japanese Americans to value their Japanese "roots" while the Japanese could appreciate the accomplishments of their American descendants across the Pacific. This could lead to collaboration in business, education and yes, diplomacy. What surprised me was the caliber of the people we met.

We're not talking about the local Kiwanis president/car dealership owner here, but people like Taro Kono, a member of the Diet, similar to a congressman in the U.S. After the formal office visit, Kono-san loved to take the JALD delegates to dinner to meet fellow members of the Diet and then out for karaoke. Kono-san's song of choice is "Hey Jude," which is a source of constant teasing from each JALD class who's heard him sing it. He attended Georgetown University, so his English is great. Whenever he was in Seattle, some of us would take him out for coffee and talk sports. Prime Minister Shinzo Abe made him minister of foreign affairs in 2017 and then minister of defense in 2019. I chuckle at the thought of how we sang karaoke with the Japanese equivalent of the secretary of state and defense!

During our trip, we also met the head of the Ministry of Foreign Affairs (MOFA) similar to the secretary of state in the U.S., and executives of the fabled Keidanren (Japanese Business Federation) who set corporate policies for the nation. I gave a short talk about being Japanese and becoming Miss Teenage America before another business group, Century 21. They laughed when I told them about the incredulous school boys at the Japanese supermarket who couldn't believe Miss

Teenage America could look Japanese and not have blond hair or blue eyes.

A highlight of the trip was meeting Princess Takamado at her residence inside the Imperial Palace grounds. The princess graduated from Cambridge University in the U.K. and was married to Emperor Akihito's cousin, Prince Takamado. The couple enjoyed traveling on behalf of the royal family. The Princess told us she loved learning about other places and cultures, including the U.S. She thought it strange that person-to-person ties between Japanese and Japanese Americans weren't as strong as one would expect. "That's why I will always meet with Japanese Americans, especially ones introduced by Hirano-san," the princess said. A woman in our delegation presented her with a gift and began to weep. "It is such an honor to meet you," she whispered. "I am so glad to hear that you appreciate the Japanese who are now Americans."

It was my "Aha!" moment.

As I mentioned earlier, growing up, my mom often complained that the Japanese looked down on Japanese Americans. When I asked her why, she complained, "They think they're better than us. They think we are all farmers. Well, when we first came here, we were, but not anymore. They criticize the way we speak Japanese. Well, we're Americans! So why should we speak perfect Japanese?"

I thought about mom, the daughter of a picture bride, and how much the Nisei and their parents' accomplished in just fifty to sixty years. It must have been frustrating for them to be invisible to their countrymen back home. It was as if they ceased to exist once they left Japan. Japanese American successes should have been a point of pride, but they weren't a point at all.

Which brings me back to Ambassador Fujisaki. In 2008, he had just started his assignment as ambassador to the U.S. after stints as Japanese ambassador to the United Nations and the World Trade Organization. He was invited by Irene Hirano to be a guest speaker at a JALD reunion at the consul general's home in San Francisco. In his talk, he gave an impassioned plea for more people-to-people programs like JALD so the Japanese could meet Japanese Americans.

"Only then will they appreciate all that the Japanese Americans have accomplished. Only then will they appreciate their brothers and sisters across the Pacific," Fujisaki said.

My jaw dropped. This was the first high-ranking Japanese official I'd ever heard who praised Japanese Americans! Perhaps we were not the scorned and forgotten people I thought we were. I made it a point to introduce myself to the ambassador and express how moved I was to hear that Americans of Japanese ancestry were appreciated, if not by the Japanese masses, at least by some in the diplomatic corps. Fujisaki-san, it turns out, went to Catharine Blaine Middle School in Seattle when his father was the consul general. He also went to graduate school at Stanford University. His experience living and going to school in the U.S. no doubt informed his knowledge of Americans in general and Japanese Americans in particular. We have been friends ever since.

I'll never know for sure what sort of crazy machinery was churning behind the scenes, but through Ambassador Fujisaki, JALD, the Japan Foundation New York, the Center for Global Partnership, Irene Hirano, the JCCCW and the Japanese Consulate staff in Seattle, I embarked on what I call my "Diplomat-Reporter At Large" period. Beginning with the JALD trip in 2005, I was tapped over and again to tell the stories of the Japanese, Japanese Americans and Seattle's J-A community both here and abroad. It was, I believe, making people-to-people relationships a reality.

In August 2010, the Japan Foundation New York and the Center for Global Partnership arranged a multi-city tour of Brazil. My assignment, which came out of the blue, was to share the Japanese American experience in the U.S. My talking points were about Japanese immigration to the U.S., the wartime incarceration on the West Coast and the role of Asian American journalists in telling those stories. Communication, of course, is a two-way street. I was learning so much about the energy and accomplishments of Japanese Brazilians. (There are more Japanese living in Brazil (1.5 million) than any country outside Japan.) I gave a speech and slideshow at the University of Sao Paulo's Center for Japanese Studies where, as expected, most in the audience had never heard about the incarceration experience. They appreciated that Asian American activists and journalists also covered groundbreaking stories of the civil rights struggle faced by people of color like the 1982 murder of Vincent Chin in Detroit.

I realized Japanese who immigrated to the U.S. and Brazil share similar histories and would be praised and appreciated by the Japanese in Japan — if only they knew their stories.

Take Sao Paulo, for example. It has the largest concentration of Japanese of all Brazilian cities, which makes for some unusual, even amusing, combinations. Names for example. Our driver was Pedro Hika, which is the Portuguese way to say Higa, an Okinawan name. A well-regarded journalist, Jorge Okubaro, may have originally been named Okubo. A sign over a restaurant downtown blared out "Kaisen Alimentos" (seafood). Simply having a conversation at the Japanese Immigration Museum involved knowledge of Japanese, Portuguese and English (English being the least spoken language in that part of the city)! A visit to the Okinawa Festival in the nearby town of Villa Carrao made me feel right at home! Like the *bon odori* festival in Seattle, families representing a wide mix of ethnicities were dancing outdoors in a large circle. They wore *yukata* and *hapi* coats. They used the same steps and arm gestures as we did dancing "Tanko Bushi" (the coal miner's dance). They even listened to the same, slightly scratchy recording of the singer warbling *"Tsuki ga deta deta ..."* The faces told the history of Brazilian immigration: Portuguese, Italian, Lebanese (there are more Lebanese in Brazil than in Lebanon), Japanese and African.

There were even more "people-to-people" coincidences awaiting me in Belem. The wife of Akira Kusunoki, the senior consul there, had been an exchange student in Federal Way, south of Seattle. Satoko stayed with the family of Jim Mason. Mason was an executive at Weyerhaeuser which, at the time, did a lot of timber trade with Japan. Satoko went to Federal Way High School. She and their daughters spoke Japanese and English as well as Portuguese. She said years later, Mason and his wife both attended her wedding in Japan.

The next day, our large ferry left Belem for the two-hour trip to Amazonia. As the tree-covered riverbank passed by, I sipped coconut water out of a fresh coconut, looking forward to my next people-to-people meetup in the Amazon.

Landing in the village of Tome Acu was like being transported sixty years back to Kekaha, Kaua'i, where my dad was born. There was a definite tropical plantation vibe about it. Wooden houses were scattered between fields of palms, cashew bushes and forests. If not for disciplined mowing, most of them would be swallowed by tall grass in no time. The main building in town wasn't City Hall, but the grange hall. It was a spare, 1960s concrete structure that belied the industriousness of the Japanese Brazilian farmers in the area. My hosts told me there was phone, fax and internet service within, if I needed it.

My main host was Alberto Ke-iti Oppata, who spoke Japanese and Portuguese and a little English. The English was because he had studied at ... drum roll please, the University of Washington's Japan Business School! He told me a hilarious story of how he thought the school was in Washington D.C. So imagine his surprise when he stepped off the plane to see, not the Capitol Building, but Mount Rainier!

Possibly in his late thirties, he looked a lot like a cousin of mine. We took a moment to analyze his name. Ke-iti was probably the Portuguese way to say his Japanese first name, Keichi. And Oppata was a form of his original family name, Ogata.

Alberto was the first Sansei president of a co-op called Associacao Cultural e Fomento Agricola de Tome Acu. He and some fellow farmers took me to their processing plant, which produces three thousand metric tons of frozen fruit pulp a year. Acai, guarana, passion fruit, cupuacu, starfruit and all manner of tropical fruit are grown here, as well as cacao and cashews.

Alberto said the co-op was doing groundbreaking research, developing a sustainable type of farming that can save the rainforest and avoid the slash and burn system of the past. He introduced me to his fellow farmer, Francisco Sakaguchi, who has a demonstration farm using SAF or *sistema agroforestal*. It avoids monoculture, instead planting a variety of crops under the canopy trees.

"The canopy keeps the sun out and slows weed growth, reducing the need for herbicide," Francisco explained, with Alberto translating.

"The canopy also attracts birds that eat insects, reducing the need for insecticide. Look how tall this acai palm has grown!" he said enthusiastically. He fashioned *peconha* (ankle straps) out of palm leaves and shimmied up the tree in no time flat.

"Yikes!" I yelled. It scared me to death.

"And we can constantly rotate the crops under the canopy, so there is always something to harvest," concluded Alberto. I made a note to introduce these guys to my friend who runs a cluster of Asian grocery stores. Frozen acai and cupuacu would be a hit in the U.S.!

I made a real connection with Francisco Sakaguchi when he took me to his family home surrounded by large mango trees. It was the same rough, dark wood home his father built when he immigrated to work on a rubber plantation in Tome Acu fifty years ago. The house looked amazingly like my Grandmother Shimizu's warehouse back in Honolulu. Rectangular and sitting on high stilts, the outdoor walls were so rough, you got splinters if you ran your hand against the grain. The screen on the swinging door was rusty.

In the front of the house, Francisco's wife and his seventy-six-year-old mother were raking peppercorns on large tarps. The fruit needed three days to dry.

"We call them black diamonds," laughed Francisco.

Inside, we drank tea and Francisco told the story of working seven years in Aichi, Japan, as a *dekasegi* (worker who has left his birthplace). In 2009, a survey by Leila Bijos on behalf of the Japan Foundation found there were 320,000 *dekasegi* from Brazil working in Japan, mostly in auto plants. Francisco says he became the unofficial mayor of his neighborhood, taking care of the approximately seven hundred *dekasegi* there.

"I learned a little about manufacturing," he recalled. "And a lot about managing people." He said he thought a lot about his identity.

"I look Japanese, I speak Japanese," Francisco said, "but in my heart, I'm Brazilian."

My last city in Brazil was the capital, Brasilia. Again, I was surprised to make even more people-to-people connections while dining at the Japanese Embassy in Brasilia thousands of miles from Seattle. Sitting at our dinner table was a Brazilian journalist, Jose Floriano Filho. I asked if he had ever been to the U.S. He said he was a Fulbright scholar in the Congressional Fellowship Program and did research for a congressman named Brian Baird. I almost dropped my fork. Brian Baird represented the third district in Washington state! Also at our table was the Embassy's minister, Toshio Kunikata.

"I remember meeting you in Hawai'i, Matsukawa-san," he said. I met Kunikata-san when he was the consul general in Hawai'i four years prior. He had hosted a JALD reunion at his home. We took a photo together at our Brasilia dinner to send to our JALD friends in Hawai'i.

My last presentation was at the University of Brasilia at a conference of university professors of Japanese language, literature and culture. I was a bit nervous being among so many academics. After all, I was just a reporter. However, many in the audience who were NOT from the U.S. weren't familiar with the incarceration experience in America, so I felt I contributed to the conversation. After the session, the keynote speaker, Carol Gluck from Columbia University, came over and told me one of the journalists I had in my slideshow was her former student. Fred Katayama worked briefly in Seattle and was a strong supporter of AAJA. He reported on-air at Reuters in New York and now works for the U.S.-Japan Council.

"Will I ever meet these people again?" I wondered wistfully as I made my way to the airport for the flight home. I thought about the very last Brazilian I spoke to before I left. She was the director of the Japanese language school in Brasilia named Kimiko Sambuichi. We were casually talking during a tour of the school, and she told me she was a "penpal bride." I stopped, surprised.

"Oh, like in Hawai'i, my grandmother was a 'picture bride,'" I said.

"Yes, I just came to Brazil and married a man I had not met before," she said. "Our first house didn't have running water or electricity."

When I asked her why she came to Brazil she said, "To try a new adventure."

My heart almost burst. I was so touched. It was as if I was talking to my grandmother who came to Hawai'i at age nineteen to marry a man she had never met to "try a new adventure." How courageous these women were! So, too, all the immigrants who traveled so far from Japan for a life unknown. Drying pepper berries — "black gold" — under mango trees; raising dairy cows on the slopes of Diamond Head; surviving a stark American concentration camp; producing tons of exotic fruit pulp; assembling cars in a country where Japanese foreigners are not appreciated. I believe if the people of Japan knew how their brothers and sisters in the U.S. and around the world achieved things despite a history of racial discrimination and legal obstacles, they would be proud indeed.

CHAPTER 22
RACE AND REPRESENTATION

First lady is what they call the president's wife. It's what they called my friend Mona Locke when her husband Gary Locke was governor. So imagine my surprise when that became my title at a tiny brick church in Seattle's Central District.

My husband Larry was asked in the summer of 2012 to become an interim pastor at Grace United Methodist Church, a historically African American congregation. A few years prior, he left his job in television management to fulfill a life-long passion. He obtained his master's degree in pastoral studies at Seattle University. He agreed to be the pastor at the church until the district found a Black pastor to take the permanent position. More than seven years later, he was still the senior pastor, as the congregation would not let him go.

We jumped in with gusto. We repainted the walls in the pastor's office and trimmed back some of the shrubbery out front. Since we didn't need to live in the parsonage next door, the congregation let a church family live there at a discount in exchange for maintaining the sanctuary and lawn.

Besides giving sermons on Sundays, Larry immediately landed in the swirl of local church life. He attended and officiated funerals, where he was often the only white clergy on the dais. He convinced the sometimes wary church leaders to temporarily house a woman in the sanctuary after she was evicted along with her two children from a rat-infested apartment. We passed out sandwiches to the homeless along Rainier Avenue South, cheered on our team at inter-church basketball games, and I was often pressed to bust out the guitar or present a children's sermon. What a great way to revisit my favorite Bible stories and songs.

I learned so much from the congregation. There was Frances Dixon, who went by the moniker "Black Panther Mom." She was the mother of Aaron Dixon, who co-founded the Seattle chapter of the Black Panthers in 1968. Her other sons Elmer and Michael were also Panthers. She told me she welcomed the young men to meet in her home at a time when Black women like herself were followed by store security while shopping at stores like Nordstrom.

There was Elbert Moore, who worked more than thirty years for the Environmental Protection Agency then as a para-educator teaching kids to read in Renton Schools for a dozen years before retiring in 2015. He is a proud alumnus of Grambling State University in Louisiana where he studied horticulture, biology and chemistry.

"How fortunate was I to graduate from a historically Black university," Mr. Moore would often exclaim. "All the people in my family before me never had the chance." Out of gratitude for what he considered a blessing, Mr. Moore is a dedicated member of the Puget Sound Chapter of Grambling State University (GSU) National Alumni Association. Besides raising money for scholarships, the alumni try to visit each other's churches. More than a dozen came to Grace and surprised Mr. Moore one Sunday. I couldn't believe so many lived here in Seattle, so very far from Louisiana!

And Sonja Hampton, who modeled what it means to be a sister in a Black sorority. For one thing, it's for life. Sonja is a member of Delta Sigma Theta, one of the "Divine Nine" Black sororities and fraternities in the U.S. To become a Delta, one had to have a B+ or better grade point average and demonstrate public service. When the sorority was first founded in 1913, one of its first activities was marching in the Women's Suffrage Parade in Washington, D.C. It wasn't uncommon to find Sonja driving people in our congregation to medical appointments or helping them organize their finances.

"We don't need to know the sister very well or hardly at all," she said. "But we will show up to provide whatever support is needed." Births, marriages, celebrations of life, graduations and swearing-in ceremonies were important in the lives of all Deltas. When I ran into Sonja at a luncheon honoring women leaders, she said she was there to support her Delta sister. And the lesson was simply this: "It is part of our culture to support each other by any means necessary."

I felt embarrassed when they called me Ms. Lori, so I just called them the same thing back: Ms. Eleanor, Ms. Bertha, Ms. Mary, Mr. Huggins, Mr. Lampkin, Mr. Hatcher. It was affectionate and kind. The music from that tiny choir just filled my heart. And nobody could out-pray Mr. Carroll Washington during "Joys and Concerns." It was a church family that embraced us unconditionally. That such a congregation would feel the sting of racism through daily microaggressions or outright discrimination angered me. I heard their stories and how they gave "the talk" about police to their children. And yet, they persevered in hope.

This warm embrace by a church community heightened my awareness of race and representation in the media. Were their voices being heard? Were under-represented communities able to bring their stories — joyous or sad — to the public's attention? Were there continuing efforts to bring more women, people of color and LGBTQ folks into the newsroom?

This question would soon get a resounding answer.

I was totally shocked when I got a call from former City Councilmember Cheryl Chow in 2012. She said she wanted to come out as gay, publicly. And she wanted me to do the interview.

"Why me?" I asked her.

"Because I trust you. You're a member of the community and I know you'll be fair," she replied.

A former teacher, principal, Seattle School Board member and Seattle councilmember, Cheryl came from a high-profile political and entrepreneurial Chinese American family. Her parents, Edward Shui "Ping" Chow and Ruby Mar Chow, owned a restaurant called Ruby Chow's on Broadway and Jefferson. It was frequented by politicians, CEOs and entertainers. Ping did the cooking while Ruby was the hostess. Ruby became the first Asian American woman elected to the King County Council. Ping, a former Chinese opera star, was the president of the Chong Wa Benevolent Association dedicated to helping immigrants. They were both gone now. Ping had just died in 2011, Ruby back in 2008. Cheryl could now come out without upsetting them.

I knew Cheryl had brain cancer. She probably didn't have long to live. She sat on a couch in her home next to her partner, Sarah Morningstar. She looked me straight in the eye and answered every question I asked.

"When did you know you were gay?" *When I was a girl growing up.*

"Did your parents know? Did you go on dates with guys?" *Yeah, I went out with guys so my parents would think I was straight. One even asked me to marry him! But I just couldn't do it.*

"You and Sarah have been together ten years, you said. Was it hard hiding your relationship?" *Yes. We began running marathons because training was a way for us to be together in public.*

"Why are you coming out now?" *I want gay kids to feel good about themselves. I wanted them to have a role model who wasn't afraid to say, 'I'm gay and that's okay.'* (Among other activities, Cheryl coached the Seattle Chinese Community Girls Drill Team for nearly fifty years.) *If I can save one child from feeling bad or even committing suicide because they felt terrible because they were gay, then I would have succeeded in my last crusade.*

"Do you think you'll get pushback from the (Chinese) community?" *No, they can't do anything to me now. What are they going to do, kill me?*

Seven months later, Cheryl passed away. She was sixty-six years old.

Race and representation became huge in my last ten years at KING TV. As I looked around the newsroom (and the Seattle market as a whole), I was encouraged. After so many years of advocating, I was beginning to see more reporters and producers of color as well as members of the gay and lesbian communities in the office. Heck, we even saw more Asian American MEN on the air, which was so refreshing! These millennials were so different from my generation in their approach to their work. For one, they had confidence in their beliefs and themselves, especially when it came to race and representation. They did not easily concede their power to authority, if at all. Many were willing to walk away from the newsroom if managers were unwilling to give them the time to present stories they felt should be heard.

Jenna Hanchard was one of the millennials who filled me with hope. She was hired to be the Tacoma bureau chief, which meant she was not based in Seattle. Local reporters considered the assignment both a blessing and a curse — a curse because the person in the bureau isn't face to face with newsroom managers on a daily basis. This could be seen as a disadvantage if a reporter wants to curry favor with the boss and get promoted within the news hierarchy. A blessing though for someone like Jenna, who grabbed the opportunity to bring the concerns of women, people of color and Blacks in particular to the television screen.

The time was ripe. Sexual abuse allegations against movie mogul Harvey Weinstein in October of 2017 and continued racially motivated violence against Blacks since the killing of Trayvon Martin in 2012 energized the Me Too and Black Lives Matter movements. In 2016, Donald J. Trump became the U.S. president. His comments and actions made me certain he will go down in history as a supporter of White supremacy groups and decidedly against people of color.

Almost immediately upon Jenna's arrival, I noticed more people of color and women were speaking in our news stories. She made a conscious effort to be inclusive in her stories, even stories that had nothing to do with race or gender. From prices at the supermarket to zoning in the City of Tacoma to the siting of a liquified natural gas plant to the history of Black churches, the images our viewers saw looked like the people who lived in Tacoma and throughout Western Washington.

It reminded me of the days when I could interview the governor, King County executive or Seattle mayor and have my "equity" bases covered because they all happened to be people of color. Jenna and I were part of a growing group of reporters and editors quoting people of color as authorities in our reports. People of color are knowledgeable commentators, leaders, educators, experts from all areas and just plain folks living and working in Western Washington. They became a part of everyday news viewing, rather than a single-issue token making a rare appearance in the media. Jenna may have been new to the newsroom, but she was quick to persuade the managers to air a series of conversations with diverse parents on parenting and race. New hires usually didn't get to do that within the first two years of landing at KING. In fact, there were enough people of color in our newsroom that we could argue with each other, like when Jenna and I got into a blow up in the newsroom one night with our show producer, Neelish Dhere, a South Asian man!

I got an email from a mother in Edmonds in February 2018 who said her teenage son and daughter were called the "N word" and feared for their safety after an encounter outside a local bar. The teens had been taking pictures for a school project at a Jack in the Box parking lot near Harvey's Lounge. A woman who worked at Harvey's was holding a baseball bat when she told the teens to get off the property and uttered the word. Jenna interviewed the family and police. She, Neel and I got into a discussion that got longer and hotter over whether to use the phrase "racial slur" or "the N-word" as part of the report. Jenna and I were convinced we should report what was alleged and not sugar-coat anything. If the N-word, with all its profound terror and history, was what the youth said they heard, then we should say so. Neel thought it was too harsh.

"I'm going to call Cheryl (our news director) and see what she wants to do," he said.

"Neel, there's a difference between racial slur and N-word, a huge difference," I argued.

Jenna agreed, "It's a loaded word. We should be specific and say what they heard, the 'N-word.'"

Neel called Cheryl and it was decided to use "racial slur." Jenna and I were deflated, but she had to hurry back to her desk. She had a deadline to meet. I wasn't done.

"Neel, call Cheryl back! Convince her!" I pleaded. "You're a BROWN MAN for Pete's sake!" Neel said Cheryl was the news director and she made the decision.

Further discussion and consultations with news managers in the following days didn't change the decision. Almost two years after the incident, Snohomish County's newly elected prosecutor (who was White) was called before the Edmonds Diversity Commission to explain why he didn't file hate crime or malicious harassment charges or even tell them he had decided not to file.

He said there were "insufficient facts." He told them the "words and the actions did not constitute a true threat."

One of the commissioners, Mindy Woods, was quoted by Teresa Wippel of *My Edmonds News* as asking the prosecutor why a woman holding a bat and using the "N-word in a threatening manner" doesn't rise to the level of a hate crime.

Prosecutor Adam Cornell said the facts just didn't prove that racial harassment happened "beyond a reasonable doubt."

To this day I wonder if he'd say the same if he was a Black parent whose children were targets of that word and all the horror it carries in the hearts of African Americans. I wonder if he could ever comprehend such a fear.

CHAPTER 23
DISASTER BRINGS US TOGETHER

Why does it sometimes take a disaster to bring people together? Perhaps it's the extreme shock and awe that demands an immediate response, like how a reporter jumps into a news car and speeds toward a plant explosion. The year 2017 brought me again to Japan in the name of earthquake survival and preparedness. It was twenty-two years since the Great Hanshin (Kobe) Earthquake of magnitude 7.3 that killed 6,434 people. It was six years since the Tohoku Earthquake of magnitude 9.0 that, combined with the ensuing tsunami, killed nearly sixteen thousand people. There was a lot we could learn from Japan about earthquake preparedness, and I was fortunate to be invited by the City of Kobe and later, the World in Tohoku organization to observe first-hand what true resilience looked like.

I must admit, I never imagined I'd have so much fun walking among gigantic water mains, peering into sewage treatment ponds or observing roof joists and *sake* tank support systems as I did in Kobe. The biggest takeaway from Kobe was: the Puget Sound region has to get ready for the big one, for it is surely coming. My heart sank a little, realizing how we in the Puget Sound area are not taking preparedness seriously.

We were taken to the Riken Advanced Institute for Computational Science in Kobe where scientists used a super-computer (the "K Computer" — *kei* in Japanese meaning ten quadrillion) to calculate how to best evacuate the city during a disastrous earthquake. City leaders then spent the money to modify building codes, streets and highways. We learned how Kobe used billions of yen to build a system using manu-ally operated gates and gravity to trap and distribute water in the absence of electrical power. This would provide drinking water and allow firefighters to put out fires, which killed hundreds of people in 1995. What the disaster taught the people of Kobe was to be prepared and work together.

"They say that volunteerism in Japan began with Kobe," said city spokeswoman Louise Dendy.

Sixty-nine-year-old Nanami Yoshimoto is one of about 150 volunteers at the Kobe Earthquake Memorial (also called the Disaster Reduction and Human Renovation Institution). Almost all the volunteers are quake survivors.

"At first, after the earthquake, the fire and police depart-ments could not do everything," she told me. "But the community came to help." Residents learned they had to take care of themselves for at least three to five days until help arrived. And for the first time in modern Japanese history, volunteers from across the country swept into Kobe to cook, collect clothing, build temporary housing, offer haircuts and children's activities and visit the elderly.

Yoshimoto and her fellow volunteers are determined to teach residents to take earthquake preparedness seriously. They have a display of a hundred items people should pack away to survive on their own for three to five days. The city even has an annual day set aside for refreshing emergency food and water supplies. Volunteers hand out recipes that use expiring food rations.

"We cannot stop nature," Yoshimoto says, "but we can be prepared and reduce the destruction."

Our journalists tour ended in Tokyo at the Ikebukuro Life Safety Learning Center. We were put on a shaking platform to simulate a 9-magnitude earthquake that went on for forty seconds. It was terrifying and loud, like an earthquake I'd experienced in Peru in the Seventies. I held tight to the table leg to keep from getting tossed around. Even so, I bumped against one of the dining room chairs during the violent shaking. Drop, duck and hold can save your life. Washington state, get serious about preparedness!

Six months later in November 2017, I was back in Japan, making a people-to- people visit to Fukushima Prefecture. I was finally visiting the region that I failed to reach during the actual disaster in March 2011. The group sponsoring this visit, World in Tohoku, brought five diverse Americans intimately close to people still rebuilding their lives after Fukushima's "triple disaster" of an earthquake, tsunami and nuclear explosion.

Throughout the Fukushima countryside are huge black plastic bags filled with radioactive soil that's been scraped off the land. Scores of them are stacked three or four high and sit like black castle walls sometimes discreetly, sometimes not so discreetly, behind temples or along the edge of a field. I'm told they will eventually be disposed of inside the Fukushima Dai Ichi nuclear plant and covered with concrete.

Akihiro Yoshikawa was our tour guide on a bus that rumbled through a part of Fukushima called the "Difficult to Return Zone." He told us to close our windows as we drove past houses and shops overgrown by weeds and vines. We were heading to Namie town, which was welcoming back residents. The slender, forty-something Yoshikawa used to work for TEPCO (Tokyo Electric Power Company), the owner of the crippled Dai Ichi nuclear plant. He quit to be a tour guide and help resettle his hometown.

"I want to talk about the positives, not just the shade," he said. But his voice quavered a bit when he recalled how his family debated where to bury his grandfather. Near the "Difficult to Return Zone" or elsewhere?

"We are trying to encourage families to move back to the safe areas," Yoshikawa said. "I personally have a love for my *furusato* (hometown)." He said they buried his grandfather near the "difficult" zone.

In Namie, there was a Saturday fall festival in full swing. There was a rock band and a children's dance group, but only a handful of spectators. Before the triple disaster, twenty thousand people lived in Namie. Only two hundred have returned. But there is a new shopping area with a restaurant, grocery store, coffee shop and *kombini* (convenience store). I found it hopeful, yet a bit sad, as did Yoshikawa-san. He said he is determined to bring Namie's "can do" spirit back. "My friends died, but I am living. I need to share and provide learning."

Misako Suzuki, a sixty-something dynamo, greeted us in a parking lot and hustled us to her home in Fukushima City. She told us her mission is to help many of the displaced people who moved to her city find joy in their lives once more. I was amazed that she welcomed a handful of strangers into her home. We rolled out plump futon quilts onto the tatami-mat floor. This is where we would sleep. Her avocation is spinning, weaving, knitting and batting colorful yarn and thread into clothing and other novelties. An entire wall of her parlor is a set of cubbies filled with balls of colorful yarn. Over a casual dinner of chicken *karaage* at her neighborhood *izakaya*, she said since the triple disaster she has decided she will only do things that bring her joy. That, she said with a twinkle in her eye, is to share the art of spinning and weaving with others to revive appreciation for Fukushima's once legendary silk industry. We strolled over to a nearby *onsen* (public bath) and again, I was amazed that a bunch of women who had only just met, were soaking together in the steamy hot water, chatting up a storm.

The next day Suzuki-san piled us into her car for a trip to an old, traditional house on the edge of town. Among the dark walls and *shoji* walls were buckets and spindles to pull silk threads off of cocoons. Looms of several sizes were crowded together, some with emerging fabric half-finished. A dozen ladies, most of them displaced by the triple disaster, gathered to dye the silk, weave it and package it for sale in the group's tiny shop in town. But before any serious weaving took place, the women prepared a simple lunch of rice, fish and pickles. As we sat on the floor around a large, low table, I asked the ladies why they came here. Haruko Sakai shocked me when she began to cry. I immediately stopped the video on my smartphone to give her some privacy. The other women sat quietly, waiting. She said her nephew was swept out to sea on 3/11. Miraculously, he held onto a piece of Styrofoam and was rescued. But her seaside home was destroyed, and she is still so traumatized, she doesn't know if she will return.

"What I found here in Fukushima City is a community of people who care about me," Haruko-san said. "I can say that sometimes, I am even happy."

As I traveled through the Tohoku region, I was filled with appreciation for the Japanese who took time to share their lives with a random group of Americans. I did not feel, as I had for decades, that they looked down on Japanese Americans. Instead, I felt a kinship, and I hoped they felt it, too. I was a witness to people who were dealt a terrible blow but faced it without shame or apology. They were people like:

- Mizuho Sugeno of Nihonmatsu who studied at iLEAP in Seattle to learn how to turn her organic farm into a school for teens dedicated to sustainable living.

- Minoru Saito of Minamisoma who dreams of turning a local festival of samurai re-enacting a battle on horseback (*Soma Nomaoi*) into a major international tourist event.
- Tomoyuki Wada of Odaka who sometimes uses money from his own pocket to attract small businesses back to town. Odaka had twelve thousand residents before the triple disaster, but only 2,400 came back by 2017.
- Karen Taira, also of Odaka, who quit her marketing job in Tokyo and opened a bed and breakfast called Lantern House. She believes tourists want to see for themselves how Fukushima Prefecture is coming back from the disaster.
- Shinichi Chiba of Matsushima, who continues to bake *castella* in a shop that was flooded by the tsunami. The delectable sponge cake comes from a family recipe that is 130 years old. Chiba once thought he would expand his cake business nationwide but decided his true love was coffee culture. He built a coffee house overlooking Matsushima Bay where people can sit, nibble on *castella* and other pastries and drink coffee. Chiba said success doesn't mean driving an expensive car or being famous. Success, he told me, was doing what makes you happy. And for him, it was making the best *castella* he could.

What are my biggest takeaways from these trips? In the face of disaster, resilience demands that I take a step forward, no matter how small, no matter how frightened I am. And do it with a community.

CHAPTER 24
THE IMPERIAL ENTHRONEMENT

This is what Cinderella might have felt, except my invitation came in an email. Hiroaki Tojo, my friend at the Japanese Consulate in Seattle, had remarkable news. I was one of seven Japanese Americans invited to the enthronement of Emperor Naruhito and Empress Masako.

"It is a great honor. Very few people are invited to the Imperial Palace to witness this," Hiro said when I called him seconds later.

"But why, what, who …?" I stammered.

"We don't know all the details," Hiro said. "But keep the week of October 20, 2019 open!" A few days later, Hiro came to the house to hand deliver the thick, cream-colored cardboard invitations not only to the enthronement ceremony, but to a dinner hosted by Prime Minister Shinzo Abe and a court banquet at the Imperial Palace for high-ranking Japanese officials as well!

I later realized the reason I was among the chosen was my mysterious and powerful friend, Irene Hirano Inouye, president of the U.S. Japan Council. All of the seven people were somehow connected to Irene and USJC! There was former Transportation Secretary Norman Mineta, Hawaii Governor

David Ige, Congressman Mark Takano of California, Christine Kubota, a Honolulu attorney who became my partner in mischief, Los Angeles executive Thomas Iino and Irene herself.

And like Cinderella, I immediately gasped, "But I have nothing to wear!" What DO you wear to an enthronement? The Consulate office offered some advice. Definitely a long dress to the palace. A cocktail dress to the prime minister's dinner. Oh, and you'll have to pay for everything yourself.

"Wow, that would cost a lot, especially because I'd have to stay a whole week," I thought out loud.

Larry looked at me incredulously. "Are you kidding me? You have to go! This is a freaking enthronement!"

I made an appointment with a stylist at a high-end department store and shopped the internet. I ended up with an understated navy chiffon sleeved gown with rhinestone cuffs for the enthronement Tuesday, a wine-colored cocktail dress with accordion angel wing sleeves for the prime minister's banquet on Wednesday and a white sequined gown for the luncheon at the palace Friday. And although it was three months since I retired from KING TV, I invited myself onto the afternoon show to show off my wardrobe. Everyone seemed delighted. I admitted to viewers I had spent money on the dresses but went to a shoe warehouse for the accessories.

On the day of the enthronement ceremony, it rained … buckets. Japan was being swept by Typhoon Hagibis. Larry and I rode to the Ministry of Foreign Affairs building in a cab. The guard at the gate couldn't find my name on the guest list but let me in anyway when I showed him my — now rain spattered — invitation. Larry waved goodbye once he saw me enter the gate. You'd never know I was wearing spiked heels seeing how quickly I skedaddled to the building, avoiding the largest puddles.

All the North and South American guests gathered in a

little room for the bus ride to the palace. There was our USJC group, but also Japanese from Brazil, Mexico, Indonesia, Canada and Peru. The men were wearing morning coats, the tuxedos with striped gray pants and a high waisted jacket with tails like the one worn by the Monopoly guy. The women were in gowns.

No photos in or outside the palace, we were warned by the young state department types who were with us. That's when Christine Kubota and I shared a glance that said, "Oh yeah? Watch me."

We stepped out of the bus and went up the stairs of the North Entrance (*Kita-Damari*) to join the two thousand guests inside. Like something out of the Oscars, scores of photographers stood on either side of the glass doors, shutters clattering like crazy. I could just imagine what they were thinking: Who's that? Is it someone important? Snap snap, anyway! Among the guests were more than four hundred foreign dignitaries from 180 countries and thirty of us of Japanese descent from North and South America.

The reception hall of the palace is a wide open space that reminded me of a fancy hotel lobby or a department store because of the long staircase. Unlike the White House, there isn't an old-fashioned column anywhere. It's all modern and sleek with gorgeous dark wood paneling, marble floors and thick carpets. Crystal chandeliers hang under LED ceiling lights.

We were led to our seats on the east side of a large courtyard filled with fluttering banners. We were seated behind the emperor's peers: Prince Charles of the U.K. Prince Albert of Monaco, King Felipe VI and Queen Letizia of Spain as well as royalty and heads of state from Malaysia, Nepal and Saudi Arabia. I looked behind me and saw my friend Ambassador Fujisaki. We chatted briefly and arranged to have coffee after the ceremony. Across the courtyard to the west was the

Seiden or State Hall where the enthronement would actually take place.

The wait was impossibly long, so Christine and I decided to go to the ladies' room. "We can take pictures there," I giggled. While waiting in a long line of ladies in the powder room, Christine kept staring at the woman behind us.

"You look so familiar," Christine finally said. "Do you play sports?"

The woman smiled and said in English, "Yeah, soccer."

Christine's eyes got big. "Ah, Sawa-san!"

Homare Sawa, who like Cher goes by just one name — Sawa — is a former professional soccer player. She captained the Japan national team to the World Cup title in 2011 and a silver medal at the 2012 Summer Olympics. We made small talk. She said the team practiced at Stanford University, so she often traveled to the West Coast.

"Can we take a selfie?" I blurted out. Sure, she said. Which goes to show: You never know who you'll meet at the ladies' room in the Imperial Palace.

We made it back to our seats just as the enthronement ceremony was about to begin. As we gazed across the white stone courtyard, the royal family members silently glided into view wearing colorful silk robes like ones worn centuries ago and slowly entered the Seiden-Matsu-no-Ma (State Room). Inside the room were two lacquer pavilions decorated in silk and gold. The drapes on the left pavilion were pulled away, revealing the emperor in a rust-colored *gosokutai* which only the emperor may wear. He wore an incredibly tall headdress called *ryuei-no-onkanmuri,* like a swallow's tail reaching to the heavens. He held a wooden baton called an *onshaku.* Beside him in the pavilion were tables holding four ceremonial objects representing his authority: a sacred sword, a sacred jewel, the State Seal and the Privy Seal. Then the drapes on the second pavilion were pulled away, revealing the empress. She was resplendent in a twelve-layer costume with thick folds of bright chartreuse and orange. Her headdress depicted the hairstyle of the medieval court — a large helmet of hair reaching skyward with a long ponytail that swept to the floor. The crowd of 2,500 was quiet. The only sounds were the occasional gong or drum.

I considered what my immigrant grandparents would have thought of this. How amazed my grandmother would be that her granddaughter would sit in the Imperial Palace to witness this sacred ceremony 105 years after she left Japan as a teenager to marry a man in Hawai'i. She would be surprised that I even watched the unfolding ritual. As late as pre-World War II, the emperor was considered divine and those fortunate enough to be invited to the ceremony had to keep their eyes downcast, never setting eyes on his royal highness.

The emperor gave a short speech. The prime minister congratulated his royal highness then led all the guests in a *banzai* cheer. In forty minutes, it was all done. I was grateful there were several cameras that captured the enthronement live. The images were beamed into our seating area so we could see the faces and costumes of the royal family close up. It was so much better than in centuries past, where the witnesses had to kneel in the stone courtyard and not look at the emperor or empress under penalty of death!

The next day, Irene gathered our American contingent at the U.S. Embassy to meet the U.S. Charge d'Affaires Joseph Young. (He became the acting ambassador after Bill Hagerty resigned to run for the U.S. Senate.) The career diplomat, who speaks Japanese and Chinese, greeted us warmly. I brought him some children's books published by the Japanese Cultural and Community Center's adult writing group, Omoide (memories). The books included the authors' childhood memories about wartime incarceration.

I couldn't help but feel like a bit of a poser, sipping coffee with Mr. Young, Irene and Congressman Takano, chatting about getting more Japanese youth to study in the U.S. He was familiar with the U.S.-Japan Council's premier program called Tomodachi (Friend), which sponsored student exchanges between the two countries to teach leadership skills. It began after the 2011 Tohoku Earthquake and Tsunami as Japanese youth clamored to rebuild their country after the devastation. We also talked excitedly about the upcoming 2020 Summer Olympics (which were later postponed due to COVID 19). Then it was out to lunch with the minister of foreign affairs, Keisuke Suzuki, who was way younger than me. I kept thinking "This can't be happening! Here I am, eating lunch with the Japanese equivalent of the U.S. secretary of state."

That evening, we joined eight hundred guests at the New Otani Hotel for Prime Minister Abe's State Dinner. There were throngs of press photographers lining the hallways and entrances to the grand ballroom and live classical music accompanied by koto. One of the most memorable dishes of the seven-course meal was the appetizer that contained caviar and a bite-sized piece of cheese wrapped in edible gold! A literal army of waiters in black tuxedos whirred about the ballroom bringing dish after dish, pouring glass after glass of wine. For entertainment, the prime minister presented artists performing UNESCO Intangible Cultural Heritage traditions: Kyogen, Kabuki, Bunraku (puppetry) and Noh. We ran into our JALD friend, former Diet member and now Minister of Defense Taro Kono. It was the first time I'd met his wife. I also greeted Secretary of Transportation Elaine Chow who was representing the U.S. at the enthronement. "Please tell Gary (Locke) I said hello," she said.

Christine and I stalked the floor looking for celebrities. I snuck a quick shot of Prince Charles sitting next to the queen of Spain by hiding my cellphone beneath my elbow.

The final event for our delegation was the banquet at the Imperial Palace on Friday. Once more, the men wore their morning coats and women dressed in long gowns even though it was the middle of the day. There were four hundred people at this event, mostly members of parliament. We were seated only a few yards from the Imperial family. There were about a dozen royals at the head table in addition to the emperor and empress. Their daughter was there as well as several of her cousins. The young women wore perky Jacqueline Onassis type hats. Strangely, Empress Masako didn't wear a hat.

When the dishes were cleared away, waiters brought each guest a gift bag from the royal couple. Inside was a heavy white box full of fish cake, *manju* and a whole smoked fish. There was a white and gold porcelain sake cup decorated with the Imperial chrysanthemum symbol. We used it to toast the new emperor and empress. There was also a metal candy dish containing colorful *konpeito* candies.

We then took a tour of the public areas of the palace. Again, the style was sleek and modern with colorful thick carpeting and beautiful Japanese paintings on the walls. I admired the rock and bonsai gardens and the fish ponds, which wrapped around the compound. It was such a masterful mash-up of modern architecture with centuries-old traditions like rock gardens and impeccably manicured trees and bushes.

As I sank into my bus seat for the ride back to the Ministry of Foreign Affairs building, I reflected on how I felt embraced and valued by my "hosts" even though I was a foreigner. Where once I felt unappreciated by the people of Japan, I now felt the children and grandchildren of Japanese immigrants were now being seen and included in a momentous event.

A few hours later over coffee at a nearby hotel, I reminded Ambassador Fujisaki that he was the first Japanese official to express joy and pride in the accomplishments of Japanese in the Americas and around the world. "It means so much to me that officials in Japan appreciate their brothers and sisters across the Pacific," I told him.

Fujisaki-san smiled. "It goes both ways. I appreciate that Japanese Americans are proud of their heritage and hang onto it as much as they do. They are almost more Japanese (in their ways) than the Japanese! Maintaining good relations between the countries takes constant work, but it's work I am happy to do."

As I look back upon the years of being a kid in Hawai'i, to traveling as Miss Teenage America, to being a student at Stanford, to working as a wife, mother and journalist I wonder, "Why?" Why have all these amazing things happened to me? What do they mean? My conclusion is I was meant to "be there." That is all. I was meant to be where I was, at each moment. I was meant to see or be seen, be a witness or documentarian, be a teacher or student, be an American or a citizen of the world.

By being there in that cabin in Kokee, Kaua'i, I was meant to play the ukulele and sing with a group. By being there at those speech competitions, I was meant to use the spoken word to be a storyteller. By being there at the piano keyboard, I was meant to perform with the choir and learn the rigors of being on stage on time. By being there representing my country across the nation and in Japan and Peru, I was meant to perhaps inspire another young woman to get on a pageant stage and win that scholarship. I was meant to show others that an American can look like me. By being there in the clattering *Stanford Daily* office, I was meant to learn if I had a thick-enough skin to document the news and survive the critiques that sometimes follow. I was meant to be on television newscasts to inspire that girl (or boy!) of color to see someone who looked like them and aspire to a career in broadcasting. Tennis great Billie Jean King said: "If you can see it, you can be it." I was meant to help build a bridge between the U.S. and Japan in a people-to-people way. No Nobel Peace Prize for sure, but the satisfaction of being able to say, "I have a friend in Japan. I have a friend in Brazil. I have a friend in Washington, D.C." means so much more.

Did I touch a life? Or two? How gratifying is that! I was meant to appreciate and be appreciated. What the future holds is a mystery, and I know I will never cease to be astonished by it all.

EPILOGUE

The original title of this book was "Astonished" because that's how my life left me most of the time.

If I am struck down by lightning at this moment, I would die satisfied that I did my best in the time I was given. In the song "Circle of Life," Elton John sings: "Some of us sail through our troubles, And some have to live with the scars." In my time on Earth, I'd have to count myself among the lucky ones, as the scars I do have are shallow and few. I see that I stand on the shoulders of giants, many of them people of little renown, but mighty supporters of youth, the next generation, the future. Whatever they saw in me I'll never fully know. But the blessings and manna poured on me were generous and undeserved. I cannot personally repay these believers; I can only pay it forward. Each time a significant event occurred in my life I was astonished. There was disbelief, amazement, followed by gratitude. I wondered, "Why me? Why is this happening?" But I grabbed and held on for what was to come. Over the years, many young people told me they decided to become a journalist because they saw me on the news set night after night. I realized that perhaps the most important purpose of my existence was simply to "be there," as testimony, as a beacon, as a guide. Looking back, there are two threads that weave through the years — my Japanese heritage and Hawaii upbringing. Without what William Seward might describe as these "mystic chords," my life would have taken a completely different trajectory and perhaps, a less astonishing one.

Lori Matsukawa
    April 29, 2020

———

Paternal grandfather Masaji Matsukawa as a youth prior to being brought to Kaua'i in 1904 by his father, Masaroku Aoyama. Circa 1890. Credit: Matsukawa family

Maternal grandparents Shogoro and Hatsumi Shimizu were successful dairy farmers. They and their sons were spared incarceration because they were vital to the war effort. Shogoro died in 1944. Honolulu, circa 1940. Credit: Shimizu Family

Mom and Dad were public school teachers in Wahiawa when I was a youngster. Circa 1958. Credit: Lori Matsukawa

Visiting grandmother Akino Matsukawa. This was baby sister Liane's first visit to Kaua'i Grandma's plantation home. Lisa and I had visited several times. Kekaha, Kaua'i 1968. Credit: Joe Matsukawa

Joe and Florence Matsukawa with daughters (L-R) Liane, Lisa and Lori. Seattle, 1994. Credit: Lori Matsukawa

At Stanford University I majored in communication and American studies. I also worked at the *Stanford Daily* and KSZU-FM. 1975-1978

Time to hand over the title and reflect on a momentous year. Fort Worth, TX, 1974

Being chosen Miss Teenage America 1974 changed my life! Fort Worth, TX, November 1973. Credit: Associated Press

My cousin Diane Morisato split chaperone duties with my mom and Ellie McDaniel during my year as Miss Teenage America. McKinley High School, 1964. Credit: Morisato Family

Meeting the real Colonel Sanders of Kentucky Fried Chicken fame at the Kentucky Derby. Louisville, 1974. Credit: MTA, Inc.

The Dr Pepper Company was the main sponsor of the Miss Teenage America program. They opened a new bottling plant in Tone, Japan, in 1974. Credit: Dr Pepper Company

Performing a traditional Maori dance at the Miss Teenage America Pageant televised on CBS. Fort Worth, TX, 1973. Credit: MTA, Inc.

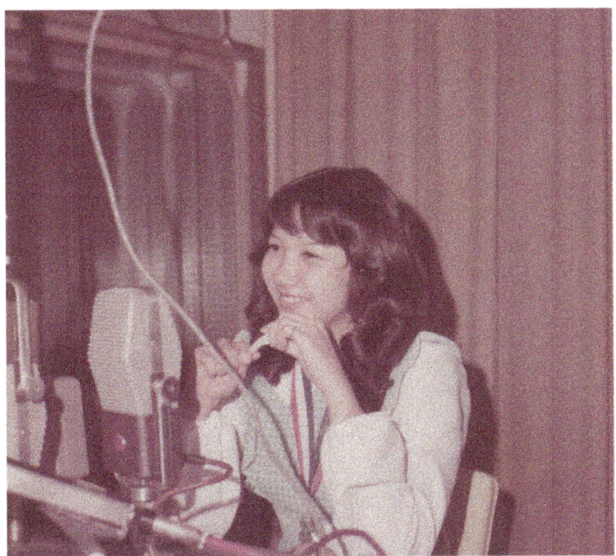

Every trip as Miss Teenage America involved interviews. That's when it occurred to me that journalism could be a good career. 1974. Credit: MTA, Inc.

Aiea High School Yearbook. Aiea, 1974. Credit: Aiea High School

Ellie McDaniel became a lifelong friend after being one of my chaperones for a year. Honolulu 1973. Credit: Aiea High School

Even after my year as Miss Teenage America, the wonderful opportunities continued to appear. Honolulu, 1975. Credit: Ralph Yempuku, Circus International

I began my career with
landline telephones and
manual typewriters using
carbon script paper.
Technology changed
dramatically over 40 years.
Credit: Lori Matsukawa

Three cities and a wedding.
Seattle, June 1982. Credit:
Lori Matsukawa

Larry, Alex and
I loved the great
outdoors. We camped,
hiked, skied and
took our motorboat
all around the
state. Credit: Larry
Blackstock

Promotional news shot featuring the news helicopter Sky KING, videographer Nancy McManus and pilot Mark Hansen. Seattle, 1990s. Credit: KING TV

One of the advantages of working the weekend shift was that I got to cover one of the biggest stories in Washington state history — the eruption of Mt. St. Helens. Seattle, 1980. Credit: KOMO TV

Honored to carry
the Olympic torch
through downtown
Seattle as part of the
upcoming games
in Vancouver, B.C.
Seattle, 2010. Credit:
Lisa Matsukawa

My first Olympics
assignment included
covering a rising star:
Federal Way short track
speed skater Apolo
Ohno. Salt Lake City,
2002. Credit: Lori
Matsukawa

Covering Governor
Gary Locke's first trade
mission to China.
Beijing, 1991. Credit:
Lori Matsukawa

I was thrilled to introduce this Japanese rookie to Seattle — Ichiro Suzuki. I told everyone, "He's the Michael Jordan of Japan." Now, everybody knows him. Seattle, 2001. Credit: Seattle Mariners

Dennis Bounds and I on the news set at the "old" KING station on Dexter Avenue N. in 2012. The station later moved to a new space on First Avenue S. in February 2016. Credit: KING TV

A truly fun photo shoot with The Tonight Show host Jimmy Fallon. Dennis Bounds and I thought he was down to earth. Seattle, 2015. Credit: KING TV

Hattie Kauffman worked at KING before heading to CBS News. Jean Enersen and I joined her for a breast cancer awareness event where she also read from her memoir about the struggles and ultimate victory of her Native American family. Seattle, 2013. Credit: Lori Matsukawa

KING TV
Covering the Vancouver Winter Olympics required numerous live-shots each day. Vancouver B.C. 2010. Credit: Ken Jones KING TV

Gordon Hirabayashi was an undergraduate at the University of Washington when his case challenging the WWII curfew went to the U.S. Supreme Court. University of Washington. Credit: University of Washington

My colleague Jean Enersen was the nation's first female weekday news anchor and worked at KING for 42 years. Seattle, 2018. Credit: Lori Matsukawa

Malala Yousafzai was the youngest recipient of the Nobel Peace Prize in 2014 at the age of 17. She survived an assassination attempt by the Taliban when she was 15 for supporting education for girls. University of Washington, July 2016. Credit: Lori Matsukawa

A career highlight: President Barack Obama awarded Presidential Medals of Freedom to three people from the Pacific Northwest whom I had interviewed during my career. Washington, D.C. November 2015. Credit: Lori Matsukawa

With Japanese Prime Minister Shinzo Abe at a US-Japan Council reception in Honolulu. He was there for a meeting with President Barack Obama at Pearl Harbor. Honolulu, December 26, 2016. Credit: Lori Matsukawa

Then-Vice President Joe Biden and I shared memories of our mutual friends, former Ambassador to China Gary Locke and his wife Mona, during his visit to Seattle to promote the "Cancer Moonshot." March 2016. Credit: Lori Matsukawa

Former U.S. Transportation Secretary Norman Mineta, me, Philippine Nikkei Jin Kai-Davao Chair Ines Yamanouchi P. Mallari, and Honolulu attorney Christine Kubota at the Imperial Enthronement. Tokyo, October 2019. Credit: Christine Kubota

Christine Kubota of Honolulu and I met Japanese soccer star (Homare) Sawa (R) in line at the ladies' room in the Imperial Palace during the Imperial Enthronement. Photos weren't allowed on palace grounds. October 2019. Credit: Christine Kubota

The Japanese Cultural & Community Center of Washington presented the former U.S. Transportation Secretary Norman Y. Mineta with the Tomodachi Award for supporting positive relations between the U.S. and Japan. Seattle, 2016. Credit: Lori Matsukawa

My first regional Emmy Award came during the final years of my television news career. It was for a series about the Japanese American incarceration and its aftermath titled "Prisoners in their Own Land." June 2018. Credit: NATAS

Consulate-General of Japan in Seattle
Receiving the Order of the Rising Sun, Gold and Silver Rays from visiting Ambassador Koji Tomita. Seattle, June 29, 2022. Credit: Consulate-General of Japan in Seattle

ACKNOWLEDGMENTS

Many thanks to those who have helped make this book possible.

To Bruce Rutledge and Yuko Enomoto at Chin Music Press who read the first very rough draft and encouraged me to continue.

To editor Anne Liu Kellor who did the heavy lifting to keep the storytelling pure and my voice present throughout.

To copy editor Katherine Kahlenberg who provided consistency, continuity and clarity.

To my "Omoide" writing group at the Japanese Cultural and Community Center of Washington who gave important feedback and encouragement.

To Barry Wong who created photographic order from chaos.

To Kelly Goto who envisioned the total package and tied it with a bow.

To friends Brenda Tome Adres, Marjorie Inn Francis, Debra Ohashi Oda, Bill Fenster and the late John Sandifer who provided details and much laughter helping me along memory lane.

To those who gave their time to read initial drafts: Gail M. Nomura, Professor Emerita University of Washington; Daniel I. Okimoto, Professor Emeritus Stanford University; author Daniel James Brown; author Helen Zia; author Jamie Ford; David Horsey, political cartoonist.

To my husband Larry Blackstock who never doubted that

I would get this work across the finish line. His love and patience are a blessing.

And of course, all the people (mentioned in this memoir or not) who gave so generously of themselves to teach a kid from Hawaii how to lead by example. By being there.